YOU COACH YOU

'This great book provides tools, ideas and inspiration to help readers seize opportunities and face new challenges. A must-read for everyone who wants to proactively seize their career' Professor Lynda Gratton, bestselling author of *The 100-Year Life*

'This is the most useful and relevant book you could buy for your career right now. No one does career development better than Helen and Sarah' Bruce Daisley, author of *The Joy of Work*

'This book will benefit everyone, whether you're just getting started in your career or are the most experienced person in the room. Sarah and Helen always have a sixth sense for exactly what people need in their careers. If you're looking for a book that makes exploring your potential and finding your way through career challenges practical and enjoyable, *You Coach You* is the answer' Kanya King CBE, founder and CEO, MOBO Group

'What I love about this book is that it gives us the tools to guide ourselves, and to know that change and true value are within us all' Mary Portas, founder and executive creative director, Portas

'In a world of endless career advice, Sarah and Helen are the real deal. They help people put themselves back in the centre of their own lives in a truly empowering and reassuring way' Emma Gannon, bestselling author of *The Multi-Hyphen Method*

'We all need this book in our lives. Helen and Sarah will help you when things get tough and find the happiness in our work that we all deserve' Holly Tucker MBE, founder, notonthehighstreet.com

'*You Coach You* has taught me that, although a lack of confidence is endemic, it's possible to coach yourself out of this fixed mindset. I'd recommend this book to anyone who's looking for more than an inspirational Instagram quote to open up their way of thinking' Eleanor Wilson, community manager, Netflix

'*You Coach You* is an opportunity to refocus on yourself and prioritize the unlocking of your potential. Read it to become more of who you really are, then read it again to become more of who you are capable of being, in all your squiggly greatness!' Amy Brann, neuroscience expert and founder of Synaptic Potential

'*You Coach You* will help you understand what's holding you back and make sure you get to where you need to be. It's a life-changer' Dr Grace Lordan, author of *Think Big*

'Sarah and Helen have a way to get right to the point and help the reader do what is needed to navigate the squiggly parts of a successful career. This is truly what self-help is all about. Finding your own path instead of waiting to be helped' Mo Gawdat, host of *Slo Mo* podcast and author of *Solve for Happy*

'Another practical and informed career manual from Sarah and Helen, rich in wisdom and good advice on taking personal control of your career development' Cilla Snowball DBE

ABOUT THE AUTHORS

Helen Tupper and Sarah Ellis are the founders of Amazing If, a company with an ambition to make careers better for everyone. They work with brands across the world, including Levi's, Vodafone, Unilever and Visa, to design and deliver practical learning experiences which help everyone confidently navigate and take ownership of their careers. Together they also co-host the UK's number one careers podcast, *Squiggly Careers*, and their TEDx talk, 'The best career path isn't always a straight line', has over one million views. Their first book, *The Squiggly Career*, was a *Sunday Times* number one business bestseller.

Prior to Amazing If, Sarah and Helen's careers included leadership roles at Virgin, Microsoft, Barclays and Sainsbury's. Helen is a trustee for the charity Working Families and Sarah is co-chair of the Mayor of London Workspace Advisory Board.

You Coach You

How to Overcome Challenges and Take Control of Your Career

Helen Tupper and Sarah Ellis

BUSINESS

PENGUIN BUSINESS

UK | USA | Canada | Ireland | Australia
India | New Zealand | South Africa

Penguin Business is part of the Penguin Random House group of companies
whose addresses can be found at global.penguinrandomhouse.com.

First published 2022

001

Illustrations by Elise Pederick
Text design and typesetting by Couper Street Type Co.
Printed and bound in Great Britain by Clays Ltd, Elcograf S.p.A.

The authorized representative in the EEA is Penguin Random House Ireland,
Morrison Chambers, 32 Nassau Street, Dublin D02 YH68

A CIP catalogue record for this book is available from the British Library

ISBN: 978–0–241–50273–0

Follow us on LinkedIn: https://www.linkedin.com/company/penguin-connect/

www.greenpenguin.co.uk

For our readers.

Thank you for choosing to spend your time with us.

We hope this book helps you whenever you need support in your career.

Contents

You Coach You   1

How to get the most from this book.

Chapter 1: How to Coach Yourself   11

Develop the mindset, skillset and toolkit you need to coach yourself.

Chapter 2: Resilience   41

Assess your current levels of resilience and how you can build your reserves every day. Identify how you can move from adversity to action when things don't go to plan.

Chapter 3: Time   73

Explore how you can take control of your time and improve the quality of your work. Move beyond busy and find the right work–life fit for you.

Chapter 4: Self-belief   117

Discover how to build your self-belief. Understand how to respond to setbacks and develop the confidence to move into your courage zone.

Chapter 5: Relationships   157

Identify the relationships you need at work and how to invest in your career community. Learn how to fix friction and repair relationships that have become difficult.

Chapter 6: Progression   193

Understand what progression means to you. Explore different progression possibilities and how to make them happen.

Chapter 7: Purpose   223

Explore what gives you a sense of direction in your career. Understand how to maximize the meaning you get from the work that you do.

Chapter 8: Advice from All Areas   255

Feel inspired by words of wisdom from Olympians, campaigners, creators, teachers and many more who have shared their best piece of career advice with us for everyone to learn from.

The End is the Beginning   283

Our careers are all a work-in-progress, there is no 'end'. A reminder to put your energy and effort into what you can control: you. And why we should all share what we know so everyone can succeed.

Acknowledgements   285
Notes   287
Index   289

You Coach You

Your career

How would you describe your career so far? 'Change', 'uncertainty', 'overwhelmed' and 'busy' are the consistent themes we hear from people in our career development workshops. Our careers are complicated, and there's a lot that we don't know and can't control. The hundred-year-old concept of a career ladder, where progress is predictable and we follow in other people's footsteps, feels outdated. Ladder-like careers no longer reflect our experiences or our aspirations. Instead, we all now have 'squiggly careers'. You will have probably already had some squiggles of your own, whether that's moving between industries or functions or perhaps changing from being employed to working as a freelancer or starting your own business. Squiggly careers give us the opportunity to explore different possibilities, define our own success and do meaningful work that matters to us. But navigating a squiggly career isn't easy. There are lots of unknowns that can leave us feeling overwhelmed and out of control. Our careers don't come with an instruction manual and at times we can feel lost, unsure where to start and in need of some support to spark our thinking.

> We need to do a better job of putting ourselves higher on our own to-do lists.
>
> **MICHELLE OBAMA**

Coaching helps us to squiggle with success

When work feels more knotty than squiggly, coaching will help you to get unstuck and to explore opportunities for the future that you find intriguing today. Coaching yourself increases the ownership and control you have in your work life and means you can design a career as individual and brilliant as you are. However, over the past few years we have frequently found ourselves grappling with what we refer to as the 'coaching catch-22'.

Coaching catch-22

If you're interested in career development, you're probably already familiar with the idea of coaching as a way of navigating the challenges and conundrums you face at work. Perhaps you are one of the fortunate few who has had a coach and experienced the benefits first-hand. We'd guess that everyone reading this book would appreciate the chance to spend one-to-one time with a career coach, and there is no shortage of coaches to fill that need. But the cost of coaching is an insurmountable barrier for most of us. Research published in the *Harvard Business Review* found that the average hourly cost of coaching in the USA is five hundred dollars. Most people will rarely, if ever, have access to a coach during their career.

Democratizing career coaching

In 2013 we founded our business, Amazing If, with a mission to make careers better for everyone. Through our podcast, workshops and our book *The Squiggly Career* we share practical ideas and actions to help people succeed in their careers. During 2020 over 500,000 people, all over the world, read, watched or listened to our work in some way. In our experience, people care about their careers and are excited about the prospect of 'squiggliness'. The people we meet are prepared to do the hard work involved in personal development but need some support with the knowledge and know-how to work through the inevitable career challenges we all experience. It's not about searching for a 'quick fix' but finding the clarity that comes from coaching and the confidence to take action.

We want to challenge the closed coaching model by sharing ideas, tools and techniques that will help you learn to coach yourself. We are both qualified coaches and believe that anyone with the right mindset and motivation can practise self-coaching to overcome challenges and make positive change. We hope this book will increase the confidence and control you have over your career and give you the chance to support other people along the way too.

The power of career conversations

This book is not intended to be a substitute for discussing your career with other people. Career conversations are helpful in all sorts of ways. Other people can provide you with perspectives you hadn't considered, support you to uncover new solutions and leave you feeling inspired to take action. These conversations could be with your manager, mentors, your work best friend, a previous colleague or someone in your family.

One good conversation can shift the direction of change for ever.

LINDA LAMBERT

We hope *You Coach You* becomes your place of preparation before your career conversations. There might be times when you can make lots of progress by yourself using the techniques and ideas we share in this book. Or maybe you'll get half-way there and can then use your awareness and insights to make your career conversations more useful and meaningful. This book might even encourage a community of like-minded learners to have career conversations together.

How to make the most of this book

Getting started

In Chapter 1, 'How to Coach Yourself', we'll cover:

Coaching mindset and skillset

We start Chapter 1 by focusing on how to develop the mindset and skillset that will support you to coach yourself through any career challenge. In mindset we'll discuss growth and fixed mindset magnets, thinking vs doing preferences and the challenge of 'critic creep'. In skillset we explore how to improve your self-awareness and accelerate your ability to listen to yourself and ask insightful questions. We recommend reading this chapter first. It will help you to get to grips with the most important principles of taking a coaching approach to your career challenges, and you'll be able to start developing your coaching mindset and skillset straight away.

You Coach You toolkit

Following coaching mindset and skillset we introduce you to our *You Coach You* toolkit, which includes thinking traps, positive prompts, coach yourself questions, ideas for action and our 'COACH' framework. These tools are designed to provide a consistent way of approaching any career challenge and you'll spot them in every chapter. Familiarizing yourself with each of these concepts and practising using them for your coaching challenges will help you to make the most of your time spent reading this book.

My coaching challenge right now

We know that you might be reading this book with an immediate career challenge in mind. In the final part of the first chapter, we have outlined the most common coaching challenges and suggested the chapters that would be most useful for you to read now and next.

You take control

In Chapters 2 to 7 we focus on how to coach yourself through the most common career challenges:

Resilience: how you respond when things don't go to plan.
Time: how you take control of your time at work.
Self-belief: how you build the beliefs that help you succeed.
Relationships: how you create the connections you need for your career.
Progression: how you move forward with momentum.
Purpose: how you develop a sense of direction and do meaningful work.

These are the coaching topics that people in our community most often come to us for support on. Whether you have an immediate challenge or not, we think it's helpful for everyone to coach themselves through these areas, regardless of experience or industry.

Each chapter follows the same structure. We begin by describing why we think each topic is an important area to coach yourself on. We then outline common thinking traps and give examples of how you can turn these into positive prompts. The rest of the chapter then focuses on how to coach yourself.

Each chapter is divided into two parts:

- **Part 1** is designed to put you on the front foot so you can invest and improve in each area continually. For example, in Part 1 of our resilience chapter you can coach yourself on how to develop your resilience reserves even if you're not experiencing a tough time at the moment.
- **Part 2** focuses on how you can overcome challenges you're experiencing in the here and now. If you're reading this book thinking *I need help now,* this is where you'll find the support you need. For example, in Part 2 of our resilience chapter if you're experiencing adversity in your career today, we will help you to coach yourself on how to work through your challenge and begin making progress straight away.

Each chapter has three closing sections:

- **Ask our expert.** We've asked someone we admire and have learnt from to provide our readers with their perspective on each topic. For example, Dan Cable, London Business School professor, shares his insights on finding your purpose and Elizabeth Uviebinené, author of *Slay in Your Lane*, gives us her perspective on building your self-belief.
- **COACH.** This is a framework to help you work through your coaching challenges. It will support you to bring together your insights and ideas into one place.
- **Summary.** Each chapter ends with a summary of the key coaching concepts, tools and questions. This will give you an at-a-glance reminder of what we've just covered and is something you can keep coming back to.

Advice from all areas

Our final chapter is called 'Advice from All Areas'. In this chapter we have asked people from all walks of life to share their career (and often life) advice, specifically for this book. Each of them has kindly offered their words of wisdom for us all to learn from. With contributors ranging from ex-England footballer Ian Wright to entrepreneur Martha Lane Fox, there is no shortage of inspiration. We can promise even five minutes spent in this chapter will leave you feeling uplifted and give you the feel-good factor we all need from time to time to become re-energized.

Reaping the rewards of your reading

The more you scribble, the more it sticks

We like seeing copies of our books looking a bit scruffy as it shows us that our work is being used and our words are useful. By making notes in this book, you'll increase the likelihood of remembering what you're learning now, for the future. The minute you start writing in this book as well as reading it, you start to make it your own. Scribbling will help ideas and insights stick in your mind and we give you full permission to make this the most scrawled-in book on your shelf.

Just keep coaching

Learning to coach yourself is not something you tick off your to-do list. It's a skill you practise, and, like any skill, the more you practise the better you get. We have repeated the exercises in this book thousands of times, for ourselves and in our workshops. We don't stand still in our careers, and as our experiences change so do the insights and the actions that you will uncover as part of your coaching approach. We recommend coming back to the exercises and tools in this book regularly to continue your development and uncover new opportunities to grow your skills.

Beyond the book

> It will come to you when you are least expecting it, while shaving or bathing, or most often when you are half awake in the morning.
>
> **JAMES YOUNG**

Coaching yourself doesn't start and end with reading or listening to this book. Our breakthrough insights and ideas sometimes happen when we least expect them: in the shower, when we're out for a walk or waiting for the bus. To make the most of this book we'd recommend being intentional about making space for these moments as part of your coaching approach. You might choose to create a ritual of reading part or all of a chapter at home, followed by some time spent in a local coffee shop to continue your reflections in new surroundings. Or maybe you read the book at the same time as a friend and after you've both completed an exercise you do a 'walk and talk' (in person or over the phone) together to chat about what you learnt.

Join the *You Coach You* community

As you work through the book, we'd love to hear about your progress and your experiences during your coaching journey. As well as our books, we create a lot of free resources full of practical tools and advice including:

Squiggly Careers podcast

We host a weekly podcast that has over 250 episodes covering every career topic you can think of, from how to make your strengths show up and stand out, to generalist vs specialist careers and how to build your self-belief.

@AmazingIf – Instagram

This is the place to go if you're looking for free career tools, tips, advice and the occasional glimpse into the behind-the-scenes reality of running a small and growing business!

Helenandsarah@amazingif.com

If you have any feedback or questions, send us an email. We'd love to hear your success stories and any ideas on what you need that we've not included or could be improved.

www.amazingif.com

This is where you can download templates to support your coaching reflections and conversations. You'll also be able to join live learning sessions if you'd like some further support with your career development.

We want you to be your best

There will be times when coaching yourself is hard work. When you wish for an easy answer or someone else who could tell you what to do. But, as the saying goes, nothing worth doing is easy, and committing to coaching yourself is investing in your career, now and in the future. As you're reading, remember we are by your side, supporting and cheering you on every step of the way. One of the best parts of writing a book is getting to know our readers, so please get in touch and let us know how you're doing. We hope you enjoy *You Coach You*, and that it supports you in your coaching and career journey.

Sarah and Helen

All you do is look
At a page in this book
Because that's where
we always will be.
No book ever ends
When it's full of
your friends.

ROALD DAHL,
'THE GIRAFFE,
AND THE PELLY
AND ME'

Coaching
isn't therapy,
it's product
development
with you as
the product.

FAST
COMPANY

1 How to Coach Yourself

What is coaching yourself?

Coaching is often described as a way of achieving an 'un' of some description, for example *un*locking potential, *un*covering opportunities, or getting *un*stuck from problems. Coaching is a skill, and skills can be learnt and practised by everyone. We define coaching yourself as:

> The **skill** of asking yourself questions to improve self-awareness and prompt **positive action**.

Your ability to coach yourself isn't determined by the level you've reached in your career, or how many years of experience you have. What matters much more is the time and effort you dedicate to continually improving your coaching skills. There is no such thing as the 'perfect coach' and we're confident that everyone reading this book will make lots of positive progress by trying out and applying the ideas that we share.

There are three areas that are useful to spend some time developing as you begin coaching yourself:

1. Your coaching **mindset**.
2. Your coaching **skillset**.
3. Your coaching **toolkit**.

In the rest of this chapter, we'll discuss each in turn, along with some actions you can take to improve your coaching ability. At the end of the chapter, we share some common career coaching challenges and the relevant chapters of the book we'd suggest you start with to coach yourself through them.

Coach yourself: mindset

Coaching yourself starts with managing your mindset. If you don't get your mindset right it's a bit like making a false start in a race: you might make some initial progress only to have to return to the beginning. In this section we explore three areas that will help you to understand your mindset: mindset magnets, thinkers and doers, and critic creep. For each area we also share actions to support you to manage your mindset as you work through your coaching challenges.

Mindset magnets

Coaching yourself is usually prompted by the motivation to make a change of some sort; it might be getting promoted, improving the relationship with your manager or something more general like looking for purpose in the work that you do. Coaching challenges are often knotty, messy and complicated. There will be times where you feel frustrated and as though you *can't* take action because the barriers are just too big. Everyone feels this way at some point in a coaching process, but it's critical that you don't lose confidence in your abilities or even risk giving up altogether.

Becoming is better than being.

CAROL DWECK

We all have what researcher Carol Dweck describes as growth and fixed mindsets. When we're in growth mindset we believe in our ability to improve, even if we haven't achieved something *yet*. In the challenging moments, we tell ourselves *I don't know how to do this, but I believe I can learn*. When we're in a fixed mindset we limit our potential and replace 'not yet' with 'not possible'. We start to believe that *I can't do this* or *this won't ever work for me* and our coaching progress can stall.

There are certain coaching situations that can act as a magnet for your fixed mindset. When you don't feel you have *control* over your context, don't believe you have the *confidence* to take action or think you haven't got the *competence* to work through your challenges, your mindset starts to work against you. Look at the diagram below. Do any of these fixed mindset magnets feel familiar for you?

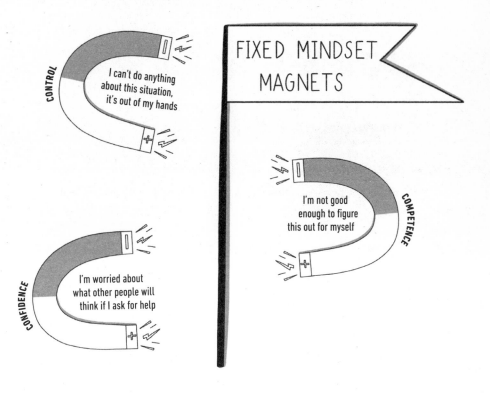

Mindset action 1: moving your mindset from fixed to growth

When you feel the pull of a fixed mindset you can consciously counteract it by recognizing moments of growth. This helps you to appreciate how you have successfully worked through challenges before and increases your confidence that you can do the same again. You will already have lots of growth mindset moments every week, you probably just don't 'label' them in that way. Take a moment now to write down and recognize a few of your growth mindset moments over the past few months:

Growth mindset magnet questions

In the past few months . . .
When have I felt in control at work?

_____

When have I felt confident in my job?

_____

When have I done something that has stretched my competence and skills?

_____

When you are working through coaching challenges it is inevitable that you will fall into a fixed mindset from time to time. When you notice the pull of a fixed mindset magnet there are two immediate actions you can take:

1. **Re-ask** yourself the questions above as this is a useful reminder that you are already spending some time in a growth mindset. Answering these questions will help you to feel positive and increase your confidence that you can move from fixed to growth.

2. **Reframe** your fixed mindset magnet by adding the word 'yet' onto the end of your thought. For example, *I can't see a solution* becomes *I can't see a solution yet*. This small tweak will prompt you to see your challenge as something to explore and learn from rather than a barrier that can't be overcome.

Thinkers and doers

Coaching yourself successfully results in both improved self-awareness and positive action. That means that you need to be a thinker and a doer at different points in the coaching process. Most of us have a natural preference towards thinking or doing, though all of us use a bit of both in our jobs.

Understanding the positives and the pitfalls of your natural style will improve your coaching and prevent you from limiting your learning or getting in your own way. For example, Sarah is a natural thinker so she is brilliant at pausing for thought but can also dwell on an idea for too long before taking action. Helen is much more of a doer, so is great at experimenting with actions quickly, but gets frustrated if her progress stalls or slows down.

In the table that follows, we've outlined the positive characteristics of each style, alongside the pitfalls and some ideas for how you can 'try on' the other approach. This is not designed to be a personality profile or to put you in a 'box'. We want you to be aware of your natural coaching style and how you can move between and benefit from both approaches as and when you need them.

Thinkers	Doers
Coaching positives	*Coaching positives*
Enjoy exploring ideas from different angles Are comfortable to 'press pause' and sit with a problem Are happy spending time thinking	Are open to experimenting quickly Enjoy taking action Value progress over perfection
Coaching pitfalls	*Coaching pitfalls*
Progress stalls in pursuit of perfection Nothing changes as no action taken Thoughts can become confused, lack clarity	Learning is something to be ticked off a to-do list Find reflecting frustrating Start lots of different things but don't always complete them
Prevent coaching pitfalls by:	*Prevent coaching pitfalls by:*
Future first. Ask yourself: *what do I want to be true in one month's time that isn't true today?* This will help you to identify actions in the here and now. **Action-its**. Get three Post-it notes, write one action on each and stick them somewhere visible. Even better if you tell someone your actions. **Doer shoes**. Who do you know who is a doer? What would they do in this situation?	**Daily ten-minute mind-map**. Set a ten-minute timer on your phone and write down all the thoughts that come into your head on your coaching challenge. **Opposite opinion**. For each of your coaching challenges consider what the opposite opinion to yours might sound like – what would that person think, say, do? **Thinker shoes**. Who do you know who is a thinker? How would they approach this situation?

Mindset action 2: your coaching preference and pitfalls

We have left space below for you to note down your reflections on your thinker versus doer coaching style, what your pitfalls might be and how you could prevent them.

<u>My coaching preference is (thinker or doer?):</u>

_____

<u>My coaching pitfalls might be:</u>

_____

_____

<u>I could prevent this by:</u>

_____

_____

Critic creep

One of the things that can get in the way of coaching yourself is when your inner critic takes control. Your inner critic is the voice inside your head that tells you that you're not 'enough' in some way. There are some examples on the next page of what your critic might sound like. We all have an inner critic, and it's fuelled by what's called our negativity bias. This is our tendency to pay more attention to, remember and dwell on the things we don't do well rather than our positive characteristics.

What does your inner critic sound like?

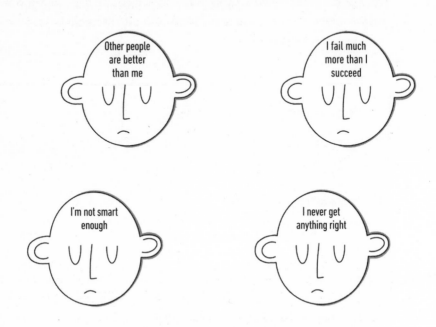

Mindset action 3: tune into your coach and calm your critic

The more we listen to our inner critic the louder and more powerful it becomes. And it's a vicious cycle – the further your inner critic creeps in, the more control it has. It prevents us from both seeing ourselves clearly and taking positive action to make progress. Next, we share two actions – be your own best friend and self-supporting statements – that you can take to turn down the volume whenever your inner critic gets too loud (and if this is a particular challenge for you, the chapter on self-belief will be useful).

Be your own best friend

Talk to yourself in the same way your best friend would. We can be our own worst critics and guilty of putting ourselves under unrealistic pressure we would never expect of anyone else. Take a minute to write down the names of three friends who support you.

My three supportive friends

1. _____

2. _____

3. _____

What is it about what these people say and how they say it that you find supportive? Perhaps they don't judge you, or help you see things clearly, or make time for you when you need it. When you're facing a coaching challenge keep these friends front of mind, so you can imagine what they'd say and listen to their supportive voices.

Self-supporting statements

Self-supporting statements are positive reminders from your inner coach on what you can achieve. They motivate you to keep going even when it's tough and leave you feeling in control, upbeat and energized. They also directly challenge negative and unhelpful thoughts you might have about yourself (quietening your inner critic). When we use self-supporting statements that are personal to us and repeat them regularly, they boost our self-esteem.[2]

Mindset action 4: my self-supporting statements

Below we've shared some examples of self-supporting statements that relate to each of the chapters in the book. Highlight any that feel particularly relevant for you. We've also left a space for you to write your own self-supporting statements, as it's important that the words feel right to you and are in your voice rather than ours. It's a good idea to write these statements in a place where you'll see them every day, maybe Post-its on a wall, or even as your laptop screensaver.

Asking for the help that I need is a sign of strength
RESILIENCE

Increasing my impact matters more than increasing my output
TIME

I build my belief by being the best version of me
SELF-BELIEF

I surround myself with people who want me to succeed
RELATIONSHIPS

I'm squiggling in a way that works for me
PROGRESSION

It's more important to make progress than to be perfect
PURPOSE

My self-supporting statements

_____

_____

_____

_____

_____

Coach yourself: skillset

Now that we've spent some time exploring your coaching mindset, we'll move on to your coaching skillset. Your mindset and skillset go hand in hand as you develop your coaching abilities.

There are three critical coaching skills that are important for every coaching challenge:

1. Self-awareness
2. Listening
3. Questioning

Coach yourself skill 1: self-awareness

Self-awareness is the most important skill to be successful in the twenty-first century at work.

TASHA EURICH

Researcher Tasha Eurich suggests that on average only around 10–15 per cent of people are self-aware.[3] This sounds like a low number but it's less surprising when you appreciate how Eurich and her team define self-awareness. They suggest there are two types of self-awareness: internal and external. Internal self-awareness is knowing our strengths, values, passions and aspirations and understanding our thoughts and feelings. External self-awareness is understanding how other people see us. For example, do you know what other people think your strengths are? Both types of awareness have significant benefits. Internal awareness increases job and relationship satisfaction and decreases anxiety and stress, while external awareness improves empathy and the ability to understand other people's perspectives. Eurich and her team also found that the two types of awareness are unrelated. Having high levels of internal awareness doesn't increase the likelihood you will have high external awareness and vice versa, so it's rare to find someone who has all-round high awareness levels.

Self-awareness = how clearly we see ourselves + understanding how other people see us

Proactively improving our self-awareness means we are better able to coach ourselves, plus we benefit from all the other upsides that Eurich found in her research. In every chapter of this book we share lots of ways you can improve your self-awareness, and below and opposite we share two more specific ideas – press pause and feedback friends – so you can get started straight away.

Self-awareness action 1: press pause

We don't get much practice at pressing pause as part of our working lives. We feel too busy with actions and tasks to take the time to stop and pause for thought during the day. And though we can blame technology, managers and work overload for getting in the way, many people find pressing pause uncomfortable. As Kate Murphy, author of *You're Not Listening*, says: *a hesitation or pause is seen as unbearably awkward and something to actively avoid*. But pressing pause, however lightly, gives us the opportunity to understand ourselves, learn more and maybe even surprise ourselves.

Finding time to press pause might sound impossible, but in reality you only need to find a short moment in a day where you can stop and ask yourself a coaching question such as:

- When did I have a positive impact in that meeting?
- What part of my day did I enjoy the most and why?
- Why do I feel uncomfortable when I talk to that person?
- Where do I feel most helpful in my job?
- When have I been at my best this week?

Asking one of these questions every day will significantly improve your internal self-awareness. It's also useful to be specific about where and when you're most likely to be able to press pause during your days. For Sarah this is when she goes on solo walks, and for Helen it's when she's making lunch.

My best time to press pause is:

_____

Self-awareness action 2: feedback friends

As you begin coaching yourself consider: *who are my feedback friends?* This is a small group of trusted people who know you well and who will be honest. This could be a mixture of people you work with today, people you've worked with previously, or even friends and family. The job specification of a feedback friend who will support your self-awareness looks something like this:

Feedback friend: job specification

- Supportive, on your side and wants you to succeed.
- Doesn't shy away from giving difficult feedback.
- Cares about you personally and can challenge you directly.
- Understands your world at work.

As an example, one of our feedback friends is the writer and podcaster Bruce Daisley. Bruce is unwaveringly direct in his feedback, and it's usually also delivered via WhatsApp. When we shared an early version of our TEDx talk his first response was *This is a bit DULL. You are interesting. This is NOT.* This feedback improved our self-awareness as it gave us insights we couldn't see for ourselves. We had worked hard on that version of our talk and felt positive about what we had created, so initially Bruce's feedback was a surprise, and we felt shocked and disappointed. However, when we revisited the talk we realized he was right. Somewhere along the way we had lost our personality in what we had written. Bruce is unflinching in his feedback and though at times that can be hard to hear, he's our number one feedback friend because there's never any doubt that he's on our side and wants us to succeed.

Use the space below to write down three people who are already, or you think could be, your feedback friends. This is a good reminder to include these people as part of your coaching process and remember to thank them along the way too. Feedback friends are a rare combination of your biggest supporters who are also brave enough to tell you the truth, so look after them well!

My three feedback friends

1. _____

2. _____

3. _____

Coach yourself skill 2: listening to yourself

How would you rate your listening skills on a scale of 1 (useless) to 10 (excellent)? In our workshops most people give themselves a score of 7 and above, though research has found that listening is a skill where we often overestimate our ability.[4] For example, Professor Ralph Nichols found that after a short talk most people missed at least half of what was said.[5] We think we're listening when in fact we're waiting to speak or distracted by something else that's happening at work. The same thing happens when we listen to ourselves. We don't finish our thoughts before we move on to the next one, or we assume we know the right

> *When you listen, you learn. You absorb like a sponge and your life becomes so much better.*
>
> **STEVEN SPIELBERG**

answer without fully exploring all the options. Practising listening to yourself (and to other people) is critical to your coaching success.

Listening to yourself action 1: interruption insight

In our conversations we frequently interrupt each other and on average we experience at least ten interruptions a day.[6] We have become used to both interrupting and being interrupted. If you want to see just how frequently both of these behaviours happen, try keeping an interruption tally in a few different meetings. We interrupt for a range of reasons, both negative (to show power or undermine) and positive (to show support and enthusiasm). Interruptions are very rarely useful as they almost always disrupt our attention. Our brains find it difficult to switch attention between tasks and this results in a division of our efforts, which reduces the quality of our thinking. These interruptions will get in the way of exploring your thoughts and uncovering new areas of awareness that can lead to those 'a-ha' insights we sometimes need to move forward.

As you begin coaching yourself watch out for when you are most likely to interrupt yourself. We've outlined some of the most common self-interruptions people experience below; highlight any that seem familiar to you and then make a note of the one that's most likely to have a negative impact on your coaching approach.

Self-interruptions

- I jump around between different thoughts and ideas frequently.
- When I've been thinking about something for a while, I get bored and prefer to move on to something else.
- I guess what the answer should be without exploring lots of options.
- If I draw a blank, I'd rather move on and answer an easier question.
- I get easily distracted by my devices.

My self-interruption insight:

_____

_____

_____

Listening to yourself action 2: dive deeper

We need to find practical ways to stay focused on our current challenge rather than moving on too quickly. Think of this as the difference between snorkelling in the sea, where you swim across the surface of the water, and scuba diving into the unknown. In every coaching challenge there will be moments where it's useful to do some scuba diving.

> *Scuba diving is how you discover the hidden treasure.*

> *Diving below the surface is when we uncover new insights about ourselves.*

To help you take the plunge, there are three different types of question that will support you in diving deeper.

Deep: focus on facts
These questions help you to gather data. They give you objective insight into a situation and sound like *Who said what?* and *What happened today?*

Deeper: focus on feelings
These questions are about your responses. They help you to understand your emotions and sound like *How did it make me feel?* and *What reaction did this trigger?*

Deepest: focus on fears

These questions can be difficult to confront. They get to the core of what's most important to you and they sound like *Why did this situation upset me?* or *Why does their opinion matter so much?*

Diving deeper

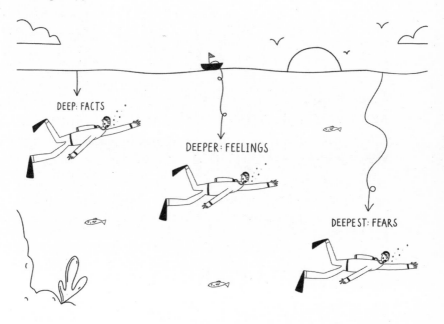

What depth of questions do you feel most comfortable with today? Deep, deeper or deepest?

Highlight which of the questions below you want to remember to include as part of your coaching approach (this might be the one you'd be least likely to ask yourself).

Facts: *How would I describe my challenge to someone using only facts?*
Feelings: *What emotions am I feeling about my challenge?*
Fears: *What am I afraid might happen if I take action?*

If I had an hour to solve a problem and my life depended on the solution, I would spend the first fifty-five minutes determining the proper question to ask . . . for once I knew the proper question, I could solve the problem in less than five minutes.

ALBERT EINSTEIN

Coach yourself skill 3: questioning

This book is full of questions to help you coach yourself. However, even better than the questions we ask you are the ones that you ask yourself. The best coaching questions are personal to you, so there is no prescribed list that you need to stick to. Before we share two questioning techniques, there are some principles to asking good questions that are a useful place to start.

The 3 Os of a coach yourself question: open, one at a time and ownership

1. Open

Good coaching questions can't be answered with a simple yes or no. Open questions start with *who, what, where, when, why* or *how*. If you spot yourself asking a closed question like *Am I committed to taking this action?* it's easy to re-ask yourself the same question in an open way: *What would increase my commitment to taking this action?*

2. One at a time

The problem with asking too many questions at once is that our brains get overloaded and we can't remember them all, let alone answer them properly. In this situation what typically happens is the last question asked gets answered and the others get lost. As part of coaching yourself you will be asking yourself lots of questions that build on each other, but you will improve the quality of your insights if you ask one question at a time. One at a time questioning helps you to generate more options and actions as part of your coaching approach. We've included an example coaching challenge here to show how this works in practice.

Example coaching challenge: You didn't get a promotion and you're not sure about how to progress in the future.

Too many at a time

| **Question:** *Why didn't I get promoted and what do other people do well that means they get promoted and what conversation do I need to have with my manager?* | **Answer:** I need to talk to my manager to see what feedback they've got and to identify when there might be another opportunity for promotion in the future. | **Action:** Arrange a meeting to get feedback from my manager. |

One at a time

| **Question:** *Why didn't I get promoted?* | **Answer:** I didn't know enough about how promotion works in this company. | **Action:** Chat to people who have been promoted previously to understand their experience. Contact HR to ask them to talk me through the process. |

| **Question:** *Who could help me with my progression?* | **Answer:** My manager, previous bosses, external mentor, recruiters. | **Action:** Reconnect with my previous manager to catch up for a coffee. |

| **Question:** *How do I stay motivated?* | **Answer:** Identify some new projects to get involved in that connect with my strengths. | **Action:** Use my next 121 with my manager to share my initial ideas and ask for their help to spot other opportunities to stretch my strengths. |

3. Ownership

Your coaching questions are all about 'I', for example: *how might I . . . ,*
what could I . . . , where will I . . . Your coaching challenges will often involve
other people, but your focus should stay on what you can control and the
actions you can take. If you find yourself blaming other people or factors
when you're coaching yourself it's a signal you need to refocus on what
you can control. When you become aware of a lack of ownership in your
coaching approach a good way to refocus back on yourself is to ask an 'I'
question that only you have the answer to. This could be *What will I do*
next? or *What have I learnt?* or *What do I feel?* The best person to come up
with solutions to your challenges is you, and by improving your self-
awareness and identifying your own actions you will be much more
motivated and committed to making change happen.

Asking yourself questions action 1: investigator and explorer questions

There will be times in the coaching process where you're not making
progress. Maybe everything feels overwhelming or too complicated to
figure out. Or perhaps you can see your situation clearly but feel stuck. We
think of this as being unable to see the wood for the trees, or being stuck
in the mud. If you feel like this at any point, try using one of the
questioning techniques below, either to get some perspective or to start
moving forward again.

Can't see the wood for the trees? Be an investigator

When we become overwhelmed by a situation it is often because it is
emotional or complicated or both. Our feelings start to take over and can
turn reflection into rumination and action into anxiety. At this stage we
don't need to worry about understanding everything and everyone
involved in the big picture, instead we need to investigate the details that
matter to us. Imagine yourself as an investigator of your situation, rather
than the person experiencing it first-hand. Looking at a situation in this
way will help you to be objective. You will understand the facts and can
then decide what to do next. Useful investigator coaching questions
include:

ℓ→ What are the facts of my current situation?
ℓ→ Who else is directly involved in my situation?
ℓ→ When do I need to make decisions?

Stuck in the mud? Be an explorer

Sometimes you might feel like you have run out of options and you start to think *I can't change this* or *I'm stuck here*. At times like this, wearing the hat of a curious explorer is useful. You care more about all the possibilities and directions you could go in, rather than worrying about how you'll get there. Useful explorer questions include:

ℓ→ Imagine if (the barrier that's getting in your way) wasn't there, what would I do?
ℓ→ What's the most ambitious action I could take?
ℓ→ How can I explore options that I might have previously discounted?

Asking yourself questions action 2: the five connected whys

Asking yourself five different but connected 'why' questions will help you get to the root cause of a coaching challenge. Each 'why' question builds on the previous one and the insights from your answers will mean you put your efforts into the actions that will make the most difference. The example below shows how this works in practice (we've kept this short and simple; your answers are likely to be longer).

The five connected whys: example	
Why 1: Why am I feeling unmotivated?	Answer: My work isn't very interesting.
Why 2: Why is my work not very interesting?	Answer: I'm not using my strengths.
Why 3: Why am I not using my strengths?	Answer: I'm in a new team and they don't know me very well or what I've done before.

Why 4: Why don't my team know what I've done before?	Answer: I haven't shared my previous experience or examples of the type of work I've done in the past.
Why 5: Why haven't I shared my previous experiences?	Answer: I don't know the best place to talk about it and I don't want to feel like I'm 'showing off' in some way.

My actions
- Have a conversation with my manager about using one of our team meetings as an opportunity for everyone in the team to share an example of their previous experience.
- In next 121 with my manager discuss how I could use one of my strengths more frequently to support our team objectives.
- Write a self-supporting statement to challenge my fear of showing off.

In this example asking the five connected 'why' questions uncovers different options and opportunities to take action. It doesn't mean the first answer is necessarily wrong, but it's only one piece of the puzzle. This example also shows that overcoming coaching challenges often involves both your mindset (feeling confident about your strengths) and your skillset (using your strengths to support your team).

Now you've spent some time developing your coaching mindset and skillset, we're going to finish the chapter by sharing our *You Coach You* toolkit. You'll find these tools in every chapter, so it's worth spending some time getting to know what they are and how they work, so you can use them to overcome your coaching challenges.

You Coach You toolkit

There are four *You Coach You* tools that you will find in every chapter. The *You Coach You* toolkit is designed to support you with any coaching challenge, so we hope this will be helpful beyond the areas we focus on in this book. We've summarized each tool on the next page so you can get a feel for what to expect and look out for in each chapter.

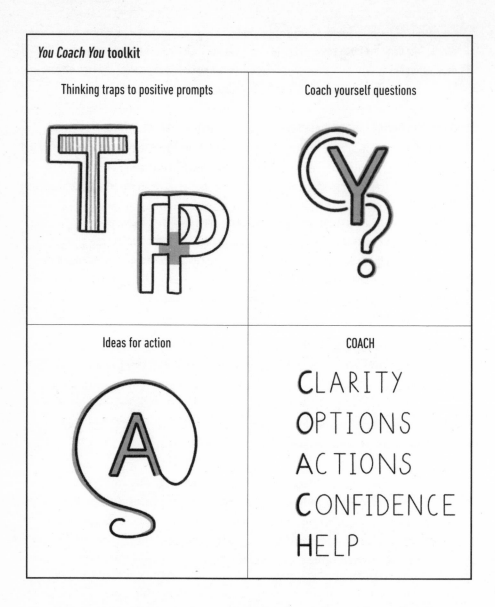

You Coach You toolkit	
Thinking traps to positive prompts	Coach yourself questions
Ideas for action	COACH CLARITY OPTIONS ACTIONS CONFIDENCE HELP

Thinking traps and positive prompts

Thinking traps are assumptions and beliefs we have that get in the way of moving forward. You can identify your thinking traps by noticing when your thoughts sound negative in some way (about either yourself or others). When we get caught in one of these traps, we can only see one solution or perhaps no solution to the problem we're trying to solve. The word 'trap' sums up how hard it can be to escape these unhelpful thoughts and they leave us feeling deflated, defensive and defeated (or even all three).

Positive prompts are how we reframe thinking traps in a way that is useful to support our coaching challenge. It might mean looking at a problem from a different perspective or viewing constraints as an opportunity to think creatively. In every chapter we share five common thinking traps for each topic and give you examples of how you can change these into positive prompts (and there are some below to bring this to life). We will also encourage you to identify your own thinking traps and practise turning them into positive prompts.

From thinking traps to positive prompts

Thinking trap: My manager is holding me back.
Positive prompt: Who else could support me in my career?

Thinking trap: There are no opportunities to progress here.
Positive prompt: How can I take control of what I want to learn?

Thinking trap: I'm not good enough for that job.
Positive prompt: What successes have I had in the last twelve months?

Coach yourself questions

As you go through every chapter, we will ask you lots of coach yourself questions. These are all open, one at a time, ownership questions which are designed to help you get unstuck and make progress. They are the questions we'd be asking you if we were in a room (or Zoom!) together. Just like the thinking traps and positive prompts, don't feel restricted to answering only the questions we ask you. As you practise coaching yourself you will find yourself coming up with your own list of 'go-to' coaching questions and there are blank pages at the back of the book if you need somewhere to jot these down.

Ideas for action

Our number one measure of success for *You Coach You* is whether reading this book helps you to take positive action. You have chosen our book for a reason, whether you're motivated to explore your potential or have a specific problem you'd like to address. Our ideas for action are suggestions for you to experiment with, adapt or use to spark new ideas rather than a to-do list. Coaching yourself is about identifying and committing to the actions that are most relevant and useful for you, and only you will know what they are.

COACH

COACH is a framework we have developed to bring together and structure your thoughts and ideas into one place (it's also a valuable tool for preparing for any career conversations you have). An important part of coaching yourself is exploring different directions, experimenting with various options and trying on new perspectives you haven't considered before.

COACH will help you with the 'so what?' of all your hard work. It brings together all your threads of thinking into one place, giving you clarity and confidence on where you are today and what you are going to do next.

COACH is an acronym that stands for:

C=Clarity
O=Options
A=Action
C=Confidence
H=Help

For each area of COACH we've outlined the purpose of each part of the framework and the sorts of questions that are useful to ask yourself (and you can add more to this as you start to practise coaching yourself).

COACH framework		
Framework	**Purpose**	**Example questions**
Clarity	What is the problem I'm trying to solve?	1. *What is on my mind at the moment?* 2. *What is my most pressing problem?* 3. *What is causing me to feel stuck?*
Options	What options could I explore?	1. *What options can I identify to make positive progress?* 2. *How else could I address this challenge?* 3. *How might other people in my (team/organization) approach this problem?*
Action	What ideas for action do I have?	1. *What actions could help me?* 2. *What feels like the most useful thing to do next?* 3. *What action would make the biggest difference to me?*
Confidence	How committed am I to taking action?	1. *On a scale of 1 to 10, how confident am I in taking the action/s identified and why?* 2. *What could I do to increase my confidence by 1 or 2 points?* 3. *What might get in my way of taking action?*
Help	What support do I need?	1. *Who could help me with my challenge?* 2. *Where else could I go to get the help that I need?* 3. *Who has helped me in the past who could help me again today?*

At the end of every chapter, you will find a blank COACH template so you can scribble down thoughts as you work through your challenge. When we're presented with a framework like COACH the temptation is to view it as something to be 'filled out' and completed in one go. In our experience COACH is most useful when you use it continually as you progress through a chapter, maybe completing one or two sections at a time. You can also revisit sections of COACH as you have new insights and ideas. We've added some spare templates at the back of the book, and you can download as many as you'd like for free at www.amazingif.com.

Common coaching challenges

We know that some readers of this book will have particularly pressing career challenges that they want to work through first. To help with this we've summarized opposite the coaching challenges we hear most frequently and recommended which chapter to start with and then where to explore next to learn more.

COMMON COACHING CHALLENGES		
COACHING CHALLENGE	START WITH . . .	THEN EXPLORE . . .
I don't get on with my manager/colleagues	RELATIONSHIPS	RESILIENCE
I want to change my job/career	PURPOSE	PROGRESSION
I'd like to get promoted	PROGRESSION	RELATIONSHIPS
I've lost motivation	PURPOSE	TIME
I want to improve my work–life balance	TIME	PURPOSE
I feel like I've stopped growing/got stuck	PROGRESSION	SELF-BELIEF
I've lost confidence in myself	SELF-BELIEF	RESILIENCE
I want to find more meaning from the work that I do	PURPOSE	PROGRESSION
I'm having a tough time at work	RESILIENCE	RELATIONSHIPS

If everything
was perfect, you
would never learn
and you would
never grow.

BEYONCÉ
KNOWLES

2 ⟿ Resilience

How you respond when things don't go to plan

Resilience: why coach yourself

1. Everyone experiences adversity during their career no matter what industry you're in, the level you've reached or how much experience you have.
2. We don't need to wait for the tough times to build our resilience. We can proactively develop the skills that will help us to respond to different types of adversity, from everyday moments of stress to the unexpected challenges that come our way.

There's no such thing as a straight line to success

You can't predict or control every aspect of your career, but you can be 100 per cent certain that there will be times where unexpected events throw you off course. Where you feel like your career is knotty rather than squiggly. Waiting for adversity to happen to us before thinking about our resilience is a risky and reactive strategy. Whereas continually and consistently developing your resilience is helpful in two ways: first, you will be better equipped to deal with the day-to-day challenges you experience in your job and, second, you will have resilience reserves ready for when you need them.

> **Resilience reserves**
> *The result of the ongoing actions you take to build your resilience so it's there when you need it.*

Adversity comes in many forms

We often associate the need to be resilient with particularly tough moments in our careers. Maybe we're made redundant unexpectedly or we find ourselves in a toxic work environment. Resilience is absolutely what we need to help us in the very hard times, though what we miss, or maybe underappreciate, is that developing resilience also helps us to navigate our everyday more successfully. In an average week at work most of us experience changing priorities, unexpected actions, new problems to solve and difficult people to deal with. When you develop your resilience, you will be able to adapt to all types of adversity, whether it's a 'tough day at the office' when a project is derailed, or the moment your hopes for the year are thrown out of the window by a company restructure. It might be helpful to think of this as your 'resilience range', how well you are able to adapt to adversity whatever form it may take.

> **Resilience range**
> *Your ability to adapt to all types of adversity, from small moments of everyday frustration to significant change.*

Resetting resilience

Resilience is commonly described as the ability to 'bounce back', but we find this description can be an unhelpful, and potentially limiting, starting point if you are coaching yourself through a tough challenge. The words we use when we coach ourselves matter. They inform, influence and impact our perspective and actions, so we should choose them carefully. As philosopher Ludwig Wittgenstein put it: *The limits of my language are the limits of my world.* In a difficult situation it is almost never realistic to go

Don't be afraid to ask for help when you need it. I do that every day. Asking for help isn't a sign of weakness, it's a sign of strength. It shows you have the courage to admit when you don't know something, and to learn something new.

BARACK OBAMA

'back' to where you were before. Framing our objective as 'bouncing back' also puts pressure on us to cope and say *I'm fine*, even if you're not. An important part of developing resilience is having the confidence to know it's OK to not be OK and to be able to ask for the help that we need. Though bouncing back is not usually meant literally, we recommend that when you are coaching yourself on resilience it is more useful to focus on the future and how you can make positive progress.

Thinking traps and positive prompts

Thinking traps are a useful way to identify any assumptions you have that could get in the way of being open and optimistic in your coaching approach.

   ↪ *I can't see a way out of my current situation.*
   ↪ *This situation feels unfair and out of my control.*
   ↪ *No one understands what I'm experiencing.*
   ↪ *I'm not a 'tough' person.*
   ↪ *I wish things were the way they were before.*

Reframing your thinking traps as positive prompts will unlock your assumptions and give you the ability to explore options and possibilities as you coach yourself.

From: I can't see a way out of my current situation.
To: What can I learn from someone who has been in a similar position?

From: This situation feels unfair and out of my control.
To: What are three 'I can' actions that would feel useful to me and are in my control? For example, I can have a conversation with a previous manager, I can update my LinkedIn profile, I can list all my successes over the past twelve months.

From: No one understands what I'm experiencing.
To: How can I share my experience in a way that will help people understand me more?

From: I'm not a 'tough' person.
To: How could I use my strengths (empathy, listening, sensitivity etc.) in a way that will help me move forward?

From: I wish things were the way they were before.
To: What am I grateful for at the moment?

My resilience thinking trap

_____

My resilience positive prompt

_____

How to coach yourself on resilience

This section of the chapter will help you to coach yourself when things don't go to plan. We want to support you to build your resilience every day, so it's there when you need it, and to give you the tools to overcome adversity in the moment.

In Part 1 we'll cover:

↪ *How to assess your resilience today, where you have strengths and where you have gaps.*
↪ *The actions you can take to build your resilience reserves.*

In Part 2 we'll focus on:

↪ *How to use an adversity audit to understand the facts of your situation.*
↪ *How to ensure your resilience reactions work for you and not against you.*
↪ *How to apply mental time-travel techniques to reflect on the past, imagine options for the future and identify actions in the present.*

This chapter finishes with our expert, Kajal Odedra, director of Change.org and author of *Do Something*, sharing her ideas on how we can become more comfortable asking for help and the value of mentors as important challengers and champions.

PART 1: Your resilience rating

There is no definitive checklist that covers every aspect of being resilient, but there are skills you can develop to build your resilience reserves. This exercise will help you to consider which ones you are stronger in, identify the gaps you have and decide the actions you want to take.

Using the scale opposite, give yourself a score between 1 and 10 for each of the following questions.

Your resilience rating

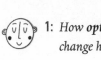 **1:** How **optimistic** am I when things don't go to plan or unexpected change happens to me?

2: How comfortable am I asking for **help**, particularly in tough times?

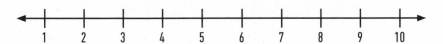

3: How often do I reflect on and celebrate my **successes**?

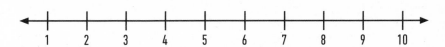

4: How confident do I feel that I have a range of people **supporting** me when times are tough?

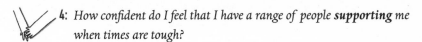

5: How good am I at **resting and recovering** during and after moments of adversity?

6: How much time do I invest in the areas **outside work** which make me feel positive and give me perspective?

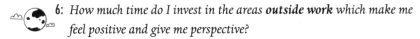

My resilience rating: .... /60
The area where I most want to improve my rating is: ....

Success isn't overnight. It's when every day you get a little bit better than the day before.
It all adds up.

DWAYNE JOHNSON ('THE ROCK')

Your resilience rating gives you an idea of how strong your resilience range is at the moment. As a reminder, this is your ability to adapt to all types of adversity, from small moments of everyday frustration to significant change. You can now use your rating to identify what actions to take to build up your reserves (the specific skills that contribute to your resilience range). On the following pages we share ideas for action and some coach yourself questions for each area of the rating to support your coaching process.

Resilience reserves 1: optimism

> Optimists aren't idiots. They do better in life – live longer, healthier, more successful lives – for the simple reason that they don't ignore problems or give up easily.
>
> **MARGARET HEFFERNAN**

Optimism feels like a personality trait, but as positive psychologist Martin Seligman has proved in his research, it is something that we can all learn to have more of.

Seligman identified three Ps (we call them the 3 Ps of pessimism) that can get in your way of being optimistic.

The 3 Ps of pessimism

1. Personal = my fault (I blame myself)
2. Pervasive = my life (nothing is going well at the moment)
3. Permanent = my future (I can't imagine things ever getting better)

Which of the 3 Ps of pessimism feels most familiar to you?

_____

We all respond to adversity differently, and no one is (or needs to be) positive all the time. Understanding how adversity impacts your optimism means you can take the right actions to make positive progress. We have suggested an idea for action for each of the 3 Ps so you can try out the one that feels most relevant for you.

Idea for action – personal: fault to feedback

Fixating on your faults doesn't help you to move forward. We all make mistakes, and no one is perfect. Sometimes other people can see our situation more clearly than we can. Asking for feedback from people who understand your experience will help you to gain perspective, forgive yourself and focus on the future. This can be as simple as describing your situation to someone and asking, *What's your perspective?*

Idea for action – pervasive: the domino effect

Write down all the different dominoes in your life at the moment, for example your family, your work projects, your interests. For each of your dominoes note one thing that's working well in each area, for example: *kids are happy at school, range of interesting clients, making time to do spin classes.* By doing this we appreciate that most of our dominoes are still standing, even if one has momentarily toppled over.

Idea for action – permanent: 1 per cent better

Start each day by writing down how you can make today 1 per cent better than yesterday. This will help you to identify small and specific ways, which are sometimes described as 'tiny nudges', to improve. Some examples of what this might look like: *read one page of a book I've been meaning to start; take a 30 min. lunchbreak; do a 10 min. yoga class on YouTube.*

CY? What actions can I experiment with if I notice my pessimism P is holding me back?

Resilience reserves 2: asking for help

In our workshops asking for help is typically the area of the resilience rating where people score themselves lowest. It seems that we would much rather help ourselves or, worse, stay stuck than burden people with our worries.

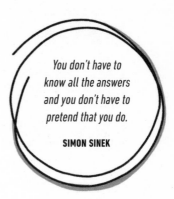

You don't have to know all the answers and you don't have to pretend that you do.

SIMON SINEK

CY? How do I feel when I'm asked for help?

However, when people are asked for help they usually feel flattered, useful, trusted and respected, which are all very positive emotions. While it might feel hard, asking for help is not something we need to apologize for or feel embarrassed about.

Idea for action: 10× help

When we ask for help, we often limit ourselves to approaching only one person. This limits our learning, because the more help you receive, the more you will gain. As the investment bank Stifel's European President Eithne O'Leary shared with us, *No one has a monopoly on wisdom.*

Imagine if we, to borrow a phrase from the world of innovation, '10×'d the help that we received. Using the table on the next page write down one career question you're curious about or stuck on at the moment. It could be anything from *How do I move into a new industry?* to *How can I improve my gravitas in meetings?* Now write down the names of ten people who could help you. Ten might sound like a daunting number but it will encourage you to seek help from different places and people. It could mean reconnecting with someone you've worked with previously or making a new connection or having a chat with your manager (or hopefully all three).

A career question I need help with:	
Ten people who could help me	
1.	6.
2.	7.
3.	8.
4.	9.
5.	10.

The coach yourself questions below will support you to be specific about the help that you need. Answering these questions will make the practical part of asking for help easier as you will be clear about exactly what you're asking for and why.

CY? What help would be useful for me at the moment?

_____

CY? Who could I ask for the help that I need?

_____

CY? Why are they the right people to ask?

_____

Resilience reserves 3: successes

When we take the time to notice the things that go right – it means we're getting a lot of little rewards throughout the day.

MARTIN SELIGMAN

When things aren't going to plan the risk of critic creep is higher. If we listen to the stories our inner critic tells us, we start to believe that we don't have any successes, or that our successes are insignificant, especially compared with other people's. The best way to get your inner coach back in charge is to start consciously spotting your successes, particularly the small ones that we all take for granted.

Idea for action: very small successes

This is one of our most popular exercises because it's easy and insightful. At the end of every day (including weekends) write down one very small success you have achieved during the past twenty-four hours. Your successes can come from any part of your life: work (updated my LinkedIn profile summary) to health (did 20 mins of boxing) to family (persuaded my toddler to eat his peas!).

To get the most from this exercise follow these three 'R' steps:

1. **R**ecognize: think about one very small success you've had today.
2. **R**ecord: write down your very small success in the same place each day.
3. **R**eflect: look back at your past successes and consider what you can learn from them.

It's particularly important that you note down your very small successes, because identifying positive moments with written words feels much more valuable than when they live in our heads as thoughts or feelings. If you're like Helen, who enjoys routines and journaling, this might be an exercise that you commit to every day. Or you might be like Sarah, who comes back to this exercise every time she finds her inner critic creeping in.

CY? How could I start reflecting on my successes in a way that works for me?

Resilience reserves 4: support system

> Anything is possible when you have the right people around to support you.
>
> **MISTY COPELAND**

Your support system is made up of the people who will help you through adversity. This is likely to be a mix of family, friends and work colleagues, past and present. When things don't go to plan it's useful to have a range of people supporting you. We all need people who support us unconditionally, and we also need people who are going to question, challenge, inspire and empathize with us. One thing to watch out for is creating an echo chamber – a support system where everyone agrees with you. You don't need to agree with someone to find their perspective useful. Sarah frequently disagrees with one of her mentors and yet she always finds his advice thought-provoking and valuable.

Idea for action: resilience role models

As we discussed at the start of this chapter, everyone experiences adversity. Consider who your resilience role models are and how you could learn from them. People can be role models for different reasons, and we've included a few examples below to get you started.

Context: Someone to learn from who has worked in a different environment from you. For example, if you're in a big company, someone who has only ever worked for themselves.

Stage: Someone at a different stage in their career from you, perhaps someone just starting out or who has retired.

Experience: Someone who has had different experiences that aren't familiar to you. For example, our friends Tom and James at The Tempest Two take on death-defying personal challenges (like climbing El Capitan) which require an incredible amount of resilience and which we can learn from even if we don't plan to start scaling sheer cliffs anytime soon!

CY? What role/s are missing from my support system at the moment?

Resilience reserves 5: rest and recovery

> If you get tired learn to rest, not to quit.
>
> **BANKSY**

Our response to adversity is sometimes to do more. We go into overdrive hoping that by working longer and harder we will get through to the other side. This approach doesn't make us more resilient, it's how we burn out. Even when we stop officially working that doesn't necessarily mean we are recovering.

Researchers Shawn Achor and Michelle Gielan found that for most of us *stopping does not equal recovering*, and the lack of recovery is what holds back our ability to be resilient and successful.[7] We all recognize the feeling of work occupying our headspace when we're having dinner with our partner or trying to sleep at night.

Idea for action: active rest

Alex Pang argues in his book *Rest* that the more we invest in deliberate and active rest the more productive we are. Active rest might sound like a contradiction, but the idea is to find activities that give your brain a rest from work by making you fully absorbed and present in something else. As Pang points out, there are lots of benefits to active rest as it helps us to 'recover from the stresses and exhaustion of the day, allows new experience and lessons to settle in your memory, and gives your subconscious mind space to keep working'. Your active rest activities are personal to you, and it's useful to reflect on how you make this part of your days and weeks at the moment. We asked some of our friends and followers on Instagram what active rest looks like for them and we've shared some examples to show how varied these activities can be; it might inspire some ideas for you too.

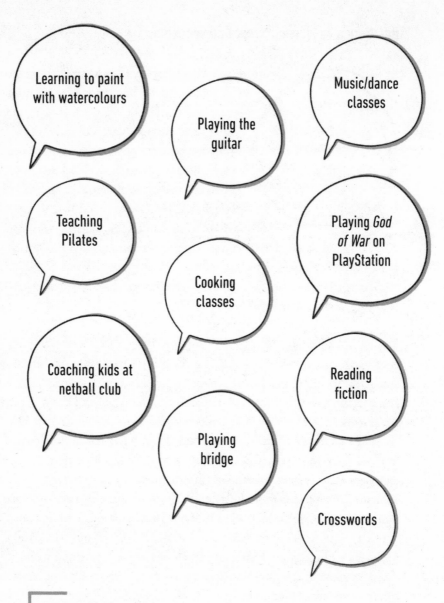

CY? What are my active rest activities?

_____

CY? How can I make active rest part of my working week?

_____

Resilience reserves 6: the world outside work

> *You don't need to make your life your job. I think you have to make time for yourself so that work doesn't become the end-all be-all.*
>
> **MEGHAN MARKLE**

Work is a big part of who we are, and a significant part of our identity is wrapped up in the work that we do. The challenge is when work becomes *all* we are, leaving no time for hobbies or people outside work. Psychologists use the term 'enmeshment' to describe the condition where our boundaries become so blurred that our individual identities lose importance.[8] If you become so enmeshed in your work that you *are* your work you are vulnerable to burnout, career crisis and losing your personality independent of the work that you do.

Idea for action: simple pleasures to make you smile

This idea is inspired by Neil Pasricha's blog *1000 Awesome Things*. Neil started his blog in 2008 at a point in his life where he was overcoming significant adversity after his marriage broke down and his best friend took his own life. He published one awesome thing every weekday for 1,000 days and they ranged from sleeping in new bed sheets to eating food you loved as a kid (you can read the list at www.1000awesomethings.com).

In the space on the next page, write down five simple pleasures that make you smile, ideally all things that are free or very low cost. Some of Sarah's are coffee, visiting National Trust gardens and reading fiction, while Helen loves cooking, a long bath and poetry podcasts. Next jot down whether you feel you are nurturing or neglecting each simple pleasure at the moment.

Simple pleasures that make you smile	Nurturing or neglecting?

This exercise gives you a quick view of whether you're nurturing or neglecting your world outside work at the moment. It might remind you that there's one thing you love that you've not done for a while or make you aware that work is dominating an unhealthy amount of your time at the moment.

CY? What areas of my life, outside work, do I want to prioritize to help me stay positive?

PART 2: How to move from adversity to action

We all react to adversity in different ways depending on both the type of person that we are and the nature of the adversity we're facing. A useful place to start when things don't go to plan is to complete an adversity audit. An audit will help you to quickly understand the facts of your challenge. This is intended to be a short exercise that will take no more than five or ten minutes, and we've included an example below to show you how this works in practice.

There is no room for facts, when our minds are occupied by fear.

HANS ROSLING

Adversity audit	
How would I describe what's happening in one or two sentences?	_____ _____ *Example: my team is being restructured and I'm not sure what will happen to my job*
How much of a surprise is this situation or did I guess/know it was coming?	_____ _____ *Example: complete surprise – didn't see it coming!*
Do I recognize aspects of this adversity (been through something similar before?) or is it a new experience?	_____ _____ *Example: been made redundant once before*

How much adversity am I experiencing in other aspects of my life at the moment?	_____ _____ *Example: life outside work is going OK at the moment*
What happens next?	_____ _____ *Example: we have a team meeting with our manager on Friday where she's going to talk to us about what next.*

The adversity audit will help you to get clarity and be concise about the facts of the situation you're facing. In moments of adversity, we feel out of control and fearful about where we are in our careers and what's going to happen next. At this time, it's easy to forget or avoid the facts of your situation. You might not agree with or like those facts, but you need to be aware of them before you can figure out what action to take. We're now going to explore how you can coach yourself on your reaction to adversity before focusing on turning your awareness into action.

Resilience reactions

Your reactions to adversity will be influenced, to at least some extent, by whether you identify as more of a thinker or doer. Thinkers will react with a desire to understand and the questions in your mind are likely to start with why: *why did this happen?* Doers' reactions are more motivated by action and their questions will start with what: *what can I do next?* Alongside your adversity audit note down your thoughts on the following coach yourself questions. It might be useful to read through the table that follows them first to support your reflections.

CY? What are my first reactions to this situation?

_____

CY? How might these reactions work for me?

_____

CY? How might these reactions work against me?

_____

CY? What can I learn from people who respond to adversity in a different way from me?

_____

Resilience reactions			
	Reactions might sound like	**Work for me**	**Work against me**
Thinkers	_I need to figure out what went wrong._ _Why is this happening (to me)?_ _I want time to think about and understand this situation._	I acknowledge and don't avoid emotions. I seek out other people's perspectives to understand more. I empathize with how other people might be impacted by my situation. I reflect on the past to learn for the future.	I can dwell on negative emotions, i.e. anger, frustration, disappointment. I can avoid action until I discover the 'right' answer.
Doers	_What can I do to fix this?_ _What action can I take today?_ _Who can help me get this sorted?_	I focus on what I can control. I feel positive that things will improve and get better. I look for ways I can take action in the here and now.	I can react first, think later. I avoid/ignore difficult emotions.

Building bridges from adversity to action

Now you can use your awareness about your current adversity to focus on what actions you want to take. We're going to explore two different exercises, both of which require some 'mental time-travel'. Time-travelling techniques are a useful part of your coaching approach, particularly when your present isn't that appealing. We'll start by reflecting on the past so you can learn from what's worked for you before. Then we will explore how imagining your future can inspire action in the present.

Resilience reflections

Reflecting on past experiences is helpful in three ways:

Time travel is always more magical somehow when you go into the past. Travelling into the future is something you do, every day. You're just not going to get very far. So, I rather like the past travel.

STEVEN MOFFAT

1. Remembering examples of overcoming adversity in the past gives us confidence that we can do the same again in the present.
2. Recalling previous adversity helps us to spot things that we are grateful for in the present and boosts our positivity.
3. Identifying how you overcame challenges helps you to consider what actions will be useful for you now.

Start by describing three examples where you have overcome adversity in the past. Aim to include different types of adversity so you can learn from the range of experiences you've had in your career so far (Sarah's examples include: *not getting promoted and being at risk of redundancy, a project I was passionate about being cancelled* and *being on maternity leave*, and Helen's: *juggling work and study, a difficult manager* and *leading people through organizational change*).

CY? What examples do I have of overcoming adversity (of any type) in the past?

Example 1: _____

Example 2: _____

Example 3: _____

CY? For each example, what actions did I take that helped me to make positive progress?

Example 1 my actions: _____

Example 2 my actions: _____

Example 3 my actions: _____

CY? What did I learn from each example that could be useful for me now?

Example 1 my learning: _____

Example 2 my learning: _____

Example 3 my learning: _____

Imagining options

You probably already have in mind at least one version of the future that is more positive than where you are today. Use the space on page 65 to jot down a few different versions of the future that you find motivating.

Without leaps of imagination, or dreaming, we lose the excitement of possibilities. Dreaming, after all, is a form of planning.

GLORIA STEINEM

The past should
be our teacher,
not our master.

ED
CATMULL

To help prompt your imagining consider:

    —↪ What's the best possible future you can imagine?
    —↪ What is a dream that feels too difficult because you don't know
        how to get there?
    —↪ What ambitions have you had before that you could bring back
        to life?
    —↪ Who are you inspired by?

Imagining my options: creating versions of my future

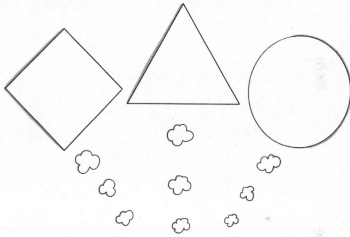

My future – version 1: _____
_____
_____
_____

My future – version 2: _____
_____
_____
_____

My future – version 3: _____
_____
_____
_____

Wishful thinking vs What next?

Imagining different futures is fun but the hard part is where to go next. Gabriele Oettingen, a psychology professor at New York University who has been studying human motivation for over twenty years, shares that, though imagining future possibilities is important, it's only effective if we also acknowledge the obstacles that could arise along the way, so we can find ways to overcome them.[9] This process of considering both possibilities and problems is referred to as 'mental contrasting'. The exercise below is designed to help you move from wishful thinking to a realistic idea for what you can do next. You can repeat this mental contrasting exercise several times to generate a list of realistic actions that you can take to help you to overcome adversity.

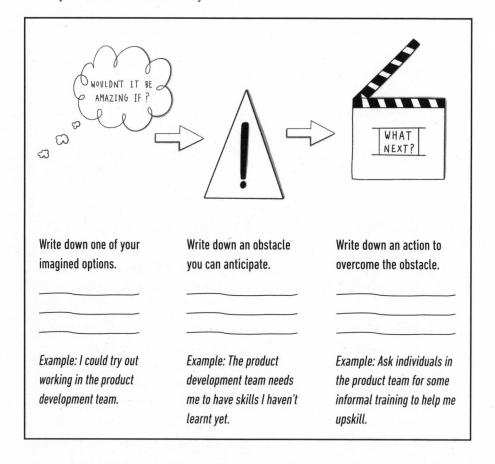

Write down one of your imagined options.

_____
_____
_____

Example: I could try out working in the product development team.

Write down an obstacle you can anticipate.

_____
_____
_____

Example: The product development team needs me to have skills I haven't learnt yet.

Write down an action to overcome the obstacle.

_____
_____
_____

Example: Ask individuals in the product team for some informal training to help me upskill.

We want to finish this chapter with a reminder that there is no ideal way to overcome adversity, no one gets it right all the time and everyone experiences obstacles in their career, even Michael Jordan: 'Obstacles don't have to stop you. If you run into a wall, don't turn around and give up. Figure out how to climb it, go through it, or work around it.'

Ask our expert: Kajal Odedra, director of change.org and author of *Do Something*

As humans we're wired to help each other.
As Helen Keller said: 'Alone we can do so little, together we can do so much.'

Coaching question: *I know I should ask for help but I'm worried people will judge me if I do and think that I should be able to help myself. What should I do?*

Expert answer: I, too, find it hard to ask for help. But whenever I have plucked up the courage to do it, I've always been so relieved that I did.

As humans we're wired to help each other
We all want to be asked to help. Think about the times when someone asked you to help them – you were probably flattered, honoured to be the person they turned to. We're social creatures who want purpose, and scientific research has found that giving activates the same parts of the brain that are stimulated by food and sex (!). Experiments show evidence that altruism is hardwired in the brain – and it's pleasurable. We get scared to ask for help because it makes us seem vulnerable and we worry it will make us look like we don't know everything. But the truth is, nobody knows everything and we all need help along the way. The smartest people are the ones that know what they don't know and seek out the information they need.

Stress can build below the surface
As a campaigner, my work can feel lonely at times. Even if you have a great community of supporters and loving friends and family, you are still the person having to make decisions and push the campaign forward. Part of the stress comes from doubting yourself, not knowing if you're making the right decisions or going in the right direction. Even if you're not conscious of this doubt, it may still be there under the surface. This low-level stress can build, and in the worst cases, make you unwell.

That's what happened to me, and the moment I realized that the source of it was the heavy burden I was carrying, I looked for a mentor. A mentor is someone who can advise and guide you. They can provide you with support through their own experience and networks. They are there to challenge you in a supportive way in order for you to grow. And most importantly, they can act as your cheerleader, someone who has the expertise and authority to tell you when you're on the right path.

Asking for help
To find your mentor, think about the people out there who are either doing similar work to you, but have more experience, or are just people you respect and admire. And ask them! Be very specific and clear on what you want out of the relationship, for example that you would like to meet them once a month for an hour to run campaign ideas past them. The worst-case scenario is that they are too busy or feel unable to take on a mentee at this time, but at least you've made the connection and they may be able to offer help in other ways later down the line. It's a flattering request for any potential mentor to be asked to help someone because of their experience or authority, so don't be scared to approach them; remember that you're giving them a compliment!

And once you have your mentor, make sure you do the heavy lifting. The mentor is giving you their time and wisdom; you need to be proactive in setting dates and coming to meetings with questions and topics you want to discuss. You will get out of it as much as you put in. A mentor is a great way of getting the support that you need without feeling like you need to pluck up courage to keep asking questions by creating a formal relationship with someone the expectation is that you will be asking for help every time you meet, which will lower the pressure. We're all a bit scared to ask for help, but we need to remind ourselves that nothing great is achieved by a single person.

You COACH You

You can use the COACH tool to bring together your thoughts and reflections from this chapter and apply them to the specific career challenge you might be facing at the moment. Taking the time to bring your insights together using COACH will help you to be clear about your actions, increase your confidence and spot the support you need. The more you practise using COACH, the more you'll find yourself using it for lots of different challenges both at work and in your career.

COACH

Clarity – what is your coaching challenge?

Options – what options could you explore?

Action – what actions will you take?

Confidence – how confident are you about taking those actions?

Help – what help do you need to overcome your challenge?

Summary

Resilience: How you respond when things don't go to plan.

If everything was perfect, you would never learn and you would never grow.
Beyoncé Knowles

Why coach yourself?	Coach yourself concepts
There is no such thing as a straight line to success; everyone experiences adversity along the way regardless of level or experience. Building resilience is something you can do every day; you don't need to wait for challenges to come your way.	**Resilience reserves:** The result of the ongoing actions you take to build your resilience so it's there when you need it. **Resilience range:** Your ability to adapt to all types of adversity, from small moments of everyday frustration to significant change.

COACHING TOOLS

Resilience rating	Imagining options
	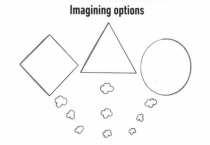

Wishful thinking vs What next?

COACH YOURSELF QUESTIONS

1. How will building my resilience help me in my job today?
2. How could I capture my very small successes every month?
3. How do my reactions to difficult situations work for and against me?
4. What have I learnt from overcoming tough times in the past that could help me in the present?
5. Who could help me when things don't go to plan?

Listen	Free downloads
Squiggly Careers podcast #143 with Martha Lane Fox	www.amazingif.com

Whatever your life brings you, respond with creation. This is the engine of resilience

ELIZABETH
GILBERT

All we have to
decide is what
to do with the
time that is
given us.

J. R. R.
TOLKIEN

3 ⟿ Time

How you take control of your time at work

Time: why coach yourself

1. We are all so busy being busy that it can get in the way of making sure our time at work is well spent. Coaching yourself will help you to move beyond busy and increase the quality of the work that you do.

2. Our work–life boundaries are increasingly blurry and aspiring to a perfect balance is unrealistic and out of kilter with our lives today. Our energy is better spent understanding the choices we can make about how we spend our time and finding our own work–life fit.

Moving beyond busy

We have all got used to answering the question *How's work at the moment?* in the same way: *Busy*. Busyness has become the accepted, and even aspired to, state of work. 'Busy-bragging' even influences our perceptions of status (of both ourselves and others). A recent study found that when looking at two different social

Beware the barrenness of a busy life.

SOCRATES

media posts, one from someone who was busy-bragging and another from someone talking about their leisure time, people believe the busy person has a higher status.[10] Having a busy and action-packed life has become a badge of honour and a sign of success.

But being busy is not the same as spending time well. Busyness leads to something that behavioural researchers refer to as 'tunnelling'. Tunnelling occurs when we can focus only on the immediate and low-impact tasks that are in front of us. This reduces the quality of our work (our IQ actually drops in this state) and leads to something called 'the time scarcity trap'. This is when we're in constant firefighting mode, which means we can't do the strategic thinking that would keep us out of the tunnel in the first place. In summary, *when we're stressed and feeling pressed for time . . . our attention and cognitive bandwidth narrow as if we're in a tunnel*.[11] Moving beyond busy is how we increase our satisfaction and feeling of 'a job well done' at work. As Cal Newport, author of *Deep Work*, says: *Do less, do better, know why*.

Finding work–life fit

The boundaries between work and the rest of our lives have become increasingly blurred over the past few years. Technology has given us the freedom to work anywhere, and at the same time has created an always-on culture. As Tiffany Jenkins writes in *New Philosopher* magazine, *we don't clock off when we are off the clock*.

> *Time management is a misnomer, the challenge is to manage ourselves.*
> **STEPHEN COVEY**

The default description of work–life 'balance' feels outdated and doesn't reflect the role work plays in our lives today. But the challenge of how work fits in with the rest of our lives remains, and we are more at risk of burning out in our careers now than ever before. The World Health Organization suggests there are three symptoms of burnout:[12]

1. Feelings of energy depletion or exhaustion.
2. Increased disconnection from your job or feeling negative about your career.
3. Reduced productivity.

If this feels familiar, you're not alone. A study by Gallup found that two-thirds of full-time workers experience burnout on the job,[13] and this negatively impacts our confidence, our performance and our health (burnt-out employees are 63 per cent more likely to take a sick day).

Instead of aspiring for 'balance', perhaps a more useful way of describing our aspiration is work–life fit. The ability to fit the different parts of our lives together in a way that works for us. This is also sometimes described as work–life flexibility and its appeal is so strong for millennials (who represent the largest generation in work today) that most would be willing to relocate to another country and be paid less in order to find it.[14]

Your time at work: well spent or wasted?

'Time' is the most used noun in the English language, which shows just how much it's on our minds. The average person spends over 90,000 hours of their life at work,[15] and as we're working for longer and retiring later that number is likely to increase. We all have the same amount of time in each day and you can't buy or make more of it. Consider what you spend

It is not that we have a short time to live, but that we waste a lot of it.

SENECA

most of your time doing at work. Meetings and emails typically spring to mind first. On an average day we receive over 120 emails[16] and spend over half of our working week in meetings, which is an increase of over 130 per cent, or thirteen hours a week, from the 1960s.[17] Two-thirds of us say we don't have time to do our jobs and end up wasting 50 per cent of our time on things that either don't help us to get the job done or don't make us feel good about our efforts.[18]

Time management myths

As you begin to consider what time well spent means to you, it's useful to address some time management myths that can get in our way.

Myth 1: there's an app for that

With all the technology we have at our disposal there must be something out there that can solve our time management challenges. A quick search in the Apple app store will offer you thousands of apps promising to do just that. While these tools can be helpful, they are unlikely to transform how you spend your time. Coaching yourself to take control of your time is challenging and the answers that you uncover will be unique to you.

Myth 2: more is what matters

Time management can feel like a search for ways to increase our output. We get up earlier, listen to podcasts at double speed and multitask in meetings. However, when output is the number one measure of how you manage your time, you'll never be satisfied (just exhausted!). We need to shift our focus from outputs to outcomes. If outputs are doing more work, outcomes are doing *better* work.

> There is a vital difference between managing time and managing work: work is infinite; time is finite. The key question to ask yourself is not 'what am I going to do?' but 'how am I going to spend my time?'
>
> **JIM COLLINS**

Myth 3: the secret to success

We're fascinated by how other people spend their time. This is partly because it's fun to get a window into other people's worlds and partly because we hope to copy their 'secrets' to success. We listen to the CEO who reads a different book each week and think *That's what I need to start doing.* A 'day in the life' interview with a successful entrepreneur prompts us to ask *Why don't I meditate for an hour every morning?* These small glimpses into other people's lives, often at their best, leave us feeling like we forgot to follow the magic formula. But there is no 'cut and paste' approach to spending your time well because we're all different and what matters is finding out what works for you.

Thinking traps and positive prompts

Thinking traps are a useful way to identify any assumptions you have that could get in the way of being open and optimistic in your coaching approach.

〜 *I have no control of how my time is spent at work.*
〜 *My days are full of back-to-back meetings.*
〜 *There aren't enough hours in the day for me to get my work done.*
〜 *Other people manage their time much better than I do.*
〜 *I don't get to spend time on the things that are most important to me.*

Reframing your thinking traps as positive prompts will unlock your assumptions and give you the ability to explore options and possibilities as you coach yourself.

From: I have no control of how my time is spent at work.
To: What helps me to feel in control in the other areas of my life?

From: My days are full of back-to-back meetings.
To: How can I contribute to a conversation or project without being involved in every meeting?

From: There aren't enough hours in the day for me to get my work done.
To: How could I work with my manager to reprioritize my work?

From: Other people manage their time much better than I do.
To: What would other people admire about how I manage my time at the moment?

From: I don't get to spend time on the things that are most important to me.
To: How could I share what's important to me with people who have an influence on how I spend my time?

My time thinking trap

_____

My time positive prompt

_____

How to spend your time well

This section of the book will help you to coach yourself on spending your time well. In Part 1 we focus on how you spend your time today and how to improve the quality of the work that you do in the time that you have. By the end of Part 1 you'll know:

- *What time well spent means for you.*
- *How to make time trade-offs.*
- *How to find your flow.*
- *How to stop distractions getting in your way.*

In Part 2 we move on to work–life fit and explore how you can take more control of the time that you have. You'll work out:

- *What work–life fit looks like for you at the moment.*
- *How to fit the different parts of your life together.*
- *How to respond when your work–life fit feels out of your control.*

We finish this chapter with ten time-management tactics for you to try out and advice from our expert, author Graham Allcott, on how to stop meetings dominating your day.

PART 1: How do you feel about your time?

Before you focus on the practical aspects of how you spend your time today it's useful to get some perspective by exploring how you *feel* about your time today.

Begin by circling how in control of your time you feel today on the scale below.

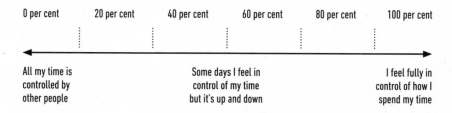

| 0 per cent | 20 per cent | 40 per cent | 60 per cent | 80 per cent | 100 per cent |

All my time is controlled by other people

Some days I feel in control of my time but it's up and down

I feel fully in control of how I spend my time

Now work your way through each of the following coach yourself questions.

CY? If I imagine my time as a person, how would I describe that person (for example, are they calm and collected, frantic and stressed, efficient and focused)?

_____

CY? When does it feel like time is flying by for me?

_____

CY? When does time feel like it's dragging for me?

_____

CY? How do I feel about my relationship with my time today?

_____

To add to your awareness, highlight the statements below that feel true for you. We've left some circles blank for any feelings that might be missing.

How do you feel about your time at work?

I feel overwhelmed
There is never enough time to do the things that need to get done.

I feel trapped
Time seems to be in charge of me rather than the other way round.

I feel guilty
I'm spending time on the wrong things or things that don't matter.

I feel out of control
Other people seem to be more in control of my time than I do.

I feel in charge
It's not always perfect but I feel in charge of how I spend my time.

I feel positive
I have worked hard to make sure my time works for me.

I feel efficient
I don't waste time on anything that isn't needed.

I feel judged
Other people don't seem to approve of how I spend my time.

I feel useful
I can see the positive impact that my time at work has.

I feel overworked
There is an unrealistic expectation of how much I can do in a day.

I feel pressured
To work in a way that doesn't work for me.

I feel torn
I divide myself up in so many ways – I wish I could be in two places at once!

I feel

I feel

I feel

How we feel about our time at work is always changing and we all have weeks where we feel overwhelmed or out of control. We'd suggest that you consider how you feel about your time at work most often. Which feelings are familiar and frequent? Before we move on to the next section jot down some thoughts on the coach yourself question below to reflect on how you *want* to feel about your time at work and try describing what time well spent means to you.

CY? How do I *want* to feel about my time at work?

Time well spent at work means

Now that you have some perspective on your time, we're going to move on to some practical tools to help you understand what you spend your time on today and decide what *trade-offs* and *trade-ups* you want to make happen.

Your task:time ratio

The purpose of this exercise is to help you quickly get a view of how you spend your time today and where you might want to make changes. The aim is not to have a 100 per cent accurate, minute-by-minute view, though there are apps like Toggl or myhours.com which will help you do that if you'd like to give them a try.

Step 1: Start by thinking about the different tasks you do at work and roughly what percentage of your time you spend on them at the moment.

My task:time ratio	
Task	**Time (per cent)**
Examples: admin, project work, learning, catch-ups, planning, emails	*Admin (10%), project work (40%), learning (5%), catch-ups (20%), planning (5%), emails (20%)*

Step 2: Now convert your table into a pie chart using the first circle opposite, so you can visualize how you're spending your time at work today.

Step 3: Use the second pie-chart circle to visualize what your ideal task:time ratio would look like.

MY TASK:TIME RATIO – TODAY   MY TASK:TIME RATIO – IDEAL

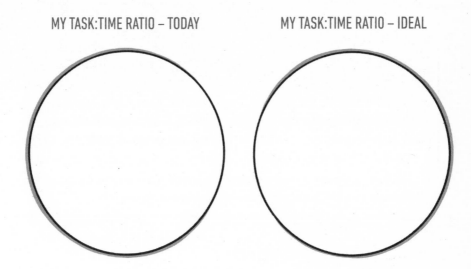

Step 4: Use the table below to summarize which activities you would like to spend more time on, which you'd like to decrease and which you're happy to stay the same.

My time at work		
Increase	**Decrease**	**Stay the same**

Time trade-offs

A common mistake when trying to change how we spend our time is to forget or ignore the choices involved in making that change happen. If you want to increase the time you spend on one activity you always have two choices: to decrease the time you spend on something else or to work longer hours to add that activity into your day. The second choice is rarely preferable or sustainable so it's more helpful to focus your efforts on becoming skilled at making 'time trade-offs'. One way to do that is by using a technique called if/then sequence statements.

If/then sequence statements

Our time trade-offs always involve choices and consequences, and if/then sequence statements help you to work out what these might be, for both you and other people, so you can identify what actions you need to take. There is no exact number of if/then sequence statements you need to work through; we would suggest you keep going until you've identified what action you are going to take next. We've included a couple of examples below to show how this works in practice and then a blank template so you can have a go for yourself.

Example 1

IF: I want to spend more time presenting
THEN: I need to spend less time co-ordinating team meetings.

IF: I want to spend less time co-ordinating team meetings
THEN: I need support from my manager to make that happen.

IF: I want to get support from my manager
THEN: I need to work out who else could help me with co-ordinating team meetings.

IF: I want help with co-ordinating team meetings
THEN: I need to consider who would benefit from the experience and skills gained from team meetings.

MY ACTION: Chat to one of my colleagues who has joined the team recently about whether they'd be interested in working with me to support team meetings.

Example 2

IF: I want to spend more time learning a new skill at work
THEN: I need to spend less time on the work I'm already doing.

IF: I want to spend less time on the work I'm already doing
THEN: I need to figure out what tasks I can stop or delay.

IF: I want to figure out what tasks I can stop or delay
THEN: I need to do a review of everything I spend time on and work out what's most important.

IF: I want to do a review of everything I spend time on and work out what's most important
THEN: I need to spend thirty minutes on a Friday reviewing my week so I can spot opportunities to reprioritize my time.

MY ACTION: Complete an audit of how I spend my time at the moment and identify what task/s I could stop that would give me a minimum of one hour a week to start learning a new skill.

If/then sequence statements	
My time trade-off:	
IF	
THEN	
IF	
THEN	
IF	
THEN	
IF	
THEN	
MY ACTION:	

Time trade-ups

> *Do first things first – and second things not at all. The*
> *alternative is to get nothing done.*
> **PETER DRUCKER**

If trade-offs are about changing how you spend your time, trade-ups are about improving the quality of the time you spend on the work that you do. In the next section we share three common time drains:

1. Failing to find your flow.
2. Managing other people's monkeys.
3. Letting distractions get in the way of making progress.

We have all experienced each of these time drains, though maybe there's one that particularly stands out for you right now. We'll explore each time drain in turn to help you identify what actions you can take to trade-up the quality of your time at work.

Time drain 1: failing to find your flow

Understanding and applying the idea of 'flow' to our work increases creativity, productivity and happiness. If you know what flow looks like for you and are proactive about finding your flow more frequently you will improve your return on time invested at work. In his book *Flow: The Psychology of Optimal Experience*, psychologist Mihaly Csikszentmihalyi describes flow as *a state in which people are so involved in an activity that nothing else seems to matter.* It feels challenging but enjoyable for us, we are 'in the zone' and fully absorbed and immersed in what we're working on, so much so that time can pass by unnoticed. The aim isn't to spend all our time in flow, as this feels unrealistic when our jobs make lots of different demands on our days. However, if we're spending all our time in the other energy states described in the diagram on the next page we risk becoming bored, limiting our learning or getting stressed.

Your four flow energy states

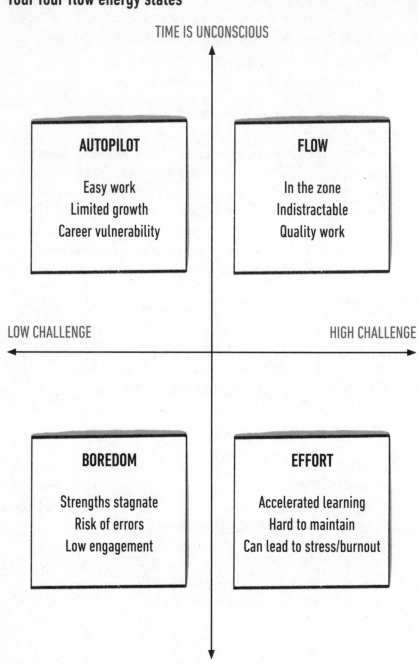

TIME IS UNCONSCIOUS

AUTOPILOT

Easy work
Limited growth
Career vulnerability

FLOW

In the zone
Indistractable
Quality work

LOW CHALLENGE   HIGH CHALLENGE

BOREDOM

Strengths stagnate
Risk of errors
Low engagement

EFFORT

Accelerated learning
Hard to maintain
Can lead to stress/burnout

TIME IS CONSCIOUS

My energy states

Consider what your energy states are at work today and number each one to show where you spend the most/least time (where 1 = most and 4 = least).

Autopilot _____
Boredom _____
Effort _____
Flow _____

Flow factors

To increase the amount of time you are spending in flow at work, there are three areas you can focus on:

1. Feeding your flow.
2. Minimizing flow foes.
3. Finding your flow friends.

1. Feeding your flow

We are more likely to find flow at work when we have a clear goal, are doing challenging work, receive frequent feedback and feel a sense of satisfaction about the work we've done. You can consciously feed your own flow by taking actions to make sure each of these four areas is in place for the work that you do. Below we've described some of the conditions that help to create flow alongside some coach yourself questions and ideas for action to support you to find more flow.

Creating the conditions of flow

Working on a project or task that you are invested in and that feels important to you. You know why you're doing the work you're doing.

> **CY?** What is one goal I am motivated to work towards in the next three months?

Idea for action: make your goal unmissable

You are most likely to lose sight of your goal when you're in the middle of a project or task, which can then slow down or even stop your flow. A useful way to keep your goal front of mind is to make it impossible to ignore. This means writing your goal down somewhere where you can't avoid seeing it before starting work, for example at the top of every page in your notebook or the first slide on a presentation.

The work you're doing uses your skills and feels stretching. We describe this type of work as feeling 'doable but difficult'.

> **CY?** How can I use my skills to make progress towards my goal?

Idea for action: help your brain to breathe

Challenging work can at times feel more difficult than doable. Particularly at the start of a project you might find yourself struggling, feeling frustrated and maybe even consider stopping. Though this feels like the opposite of flow, you should feel reassured this is part of the process of finding flow. When you reach this stage the best thing you can do is take a short break and do something to get your body moving in a gentle way, for example going for a walk, doing some gardening or even breathing exercises. During these types of activities our brains release a chemical called nitric oxide, which relieves stress, creates a sense of calm and generally helps us to feel good. Giving yourself and your brain a break will increase your chances of finding flow when you return to your work.

FREQUENT
FEEDBACK

You receive regular feedback that gives you a sense of how you're progressing. Frequent feedback keeps us focused and motivated.

CY? Who can I ask for feedback so I know I'm on the right track to meet my goal?

Idea for action: ask for www + ebi feedback

One of the most simple and straightforward ways we've discovered of asking for frequent feedback is using *what's working well* and *even-better-if* questions. For example, if you're working on a project with three other people, then at the end of every week you could agree to all share one idea for an 'even better if' for the next week. You can also ask these questions to yourself so you are taking control of your continual improvement.

This is the satisfaction and enjoyment you get from a job well done. It means recognizing your progress and what you've learnt along the way.

CY? What does a job well done look like for my goal?

_____

Idea for action: pride postcard

To recognize what you've learnt and achieved from a project or task it can be nice to create something tangible (there's a reason most of us still love a certificate or a medal!). Pride postcards are a way of writing a few short sentences to reflect on and celebrate your successes. If you are working on a goal as part of a team you could even send pride postcards to each other when you achieve your goal. We've given an example of a simple 'pride postcard' template below and you can get much more creative by designing your own digital postcard templates for free using the Canva platform.

One of the other areas that contributes to finding flow is giving all your attention and concentration to the work you're doing. We cover distraction downfalls and how to stop them getting in your way as the third area of time trade-ups and we'll come to this shortly.

2. Minimizing flow foes

Your environment plays an important part in finding your flow. Where some people find music soothing, other people find it stops their concentration. Some people feel more creative in a messy environment and other people need a clear desk. When we work out the environment that supports our flow, we can minimize the flow foes that might get in our way. This is something that looks different for all of us and thinking about where you work and how you create a space that supports your flow is important to your success.

CY? What working environment helps me to feel most in flow?

_____

CY? How can I remove any flow floes that might get in my way?

_____

Idea for action: energy ✕ environment audit

For a week track your energy and environment at work. You can do this very simply by taking thirty seconds after each task (whether it's a meeting, conversation or piece of work) to note down whether you felt low, medium or high energy and where you were at the time. After five days, review all your high-energy tasks and reflect on your surroundings for those tasks. You might notice that one day had more high-energy moments and you were working in a different way when you did them. Or maybe your high energy relates to the time of day when you complete tasks. You don't need to be in flow all the time but for your most important work you can use this audit to identify how you can change your surroundings to support your flow.

3. Finding flow friends

Finding flow is not exclusively a solo endeavour. Interdependent flow, when you're working together with others who share your passion, actually feeds our flow cycle more than working by ourselves. We get more enjoyment and reward from collective than individual feelings of flow. Your flow friends can be people in or out of your current organization, and side projects or volunteering activities are also a great way of finding your flow friends.

CY? Who do I work with that shares my passions and is committed to the same goals?

CY? How could we work together in a way that will improve our chances of flow?

Idea for action: follow your interests to find your tribe

Finding flow friends might sound difficult and daunting, especially if you're more introverted, like Sarah. If you start by following your interests, you will find that opportunities to spend time with flow friends arise naturally. Some communities are even creating specific moments for groups of people with the same passion who are in different places to find flow together. For example, the London Writers' Salon has a daily writing hour anyone can join, and Rebel Book Club is a community of people who help each other to find flow with their reading and learning.

How I'm going to find more flow

One action I'm going to take to increase the amount of time I spend in flow:

_____

Time drain 2: managing other people's monkeys

In 1974 William Oncken and Donald Wass published one of the *Harvard Business Review*'s most popular articles. It was called 'Management Time: Who's Got the Monkey?'[19] A 'monkey' is simply a job to be done, and in our day-to-day work we're all carrying around a lot of monkeys. Managing our time is more of a challenge if we find ourselves with other people's monkeys to take care of as well as our own. This might be because someone has delegated their monkey to us, or we find ourselves volunteering to take on someone else's task in a desire to be helpful. The result is we end up carrying more monkeys than we can possibly manage in the time we have available.

On the next page are some examples of typical monkey 'adopting' scenarios and a suggestion for how you could approach each situation in a different way.

Managing your monkeys

Monkey	Adopting the monkey	Managing the monkey	CY?
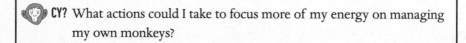 New piece of work from your manager to complete by the end of the week.	'Yes, I'll get that done no problem' (cue working late nights).	'Yes, I can support you with that. Before I start can we discuss my current priorities so we can agree what's most important to achieve by when?'	How do I agree my priorities with my manager?
Someone asks you to help them because they are stuck, and they know you've done that task before.	'Of course, I'm really happy to help, why don't I just do that for you?'	'Of course, I will help. Can you share where you've got to and we can figure out together what you might do next?'	How can I help other people to help themselves?
In a meeting someone is asked to volunteer for a task (sometimes followed by an uncomfortable silence).	'I can do that – no problem!'	Sometimes it's OK to say nothing – practise the power of the pause. Or, if that feels like a big leap from where you are now, you could try: 'I'd be happy to do that task but it would mean I couldn't do x, can we discuss which is more important?'	What am I compromising by giving away my time?

Managing your monkeys: coach yourself questions

CY? What does managing other people's monkeys look like for me?

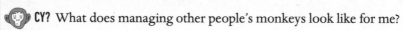

CY? How often do I find myself managing other people's monkeys?

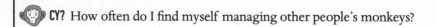

CY? What actions could I take to focus more of my energy on managing my own monkeys?

Time drain 3: distraction downfalls

There's no shortage of things competing for our attention: notifications, instant messages, emails, social media. And it's no surprise that we're attracted to these distractions as they are designed to give us short, sharp bursts of dopamine. However, the impact of disruptions is significant. They consume, on average, three hours of extra time in our day, which means tasks take 27 per cent longer to complete.[20] They also reduce the quality of the work that we do as our brains don't respond well to context switching. While we might feel we're multitasking if we keep an eye on our notifications while trying to write a presentation, the reality is our brain is actually rapidly switching from one activity to another. When our brains are in this 'skittish state' our productivity reduces.

Idea for action: find friction

Nobody does their best work when distracted, but knowing this isn't enough, as they are hard habits to let go of. It might even be useful to frame your distraction downfalls as bad habits as it reminds us they are something to 'give up'. Have a look at some of the most common distraction downfalls on the next page and tick the ones that are relevant for you. We've also left a few blanks in case there are any others that you can spot for yourself. Next, answer the coach yourself questions and be as specific as possible – so, rather than describing your distraction as 'social media' you might say *WhatsApp messages that could wait until later* (this is Sarah's example!)

Distraction downfalls

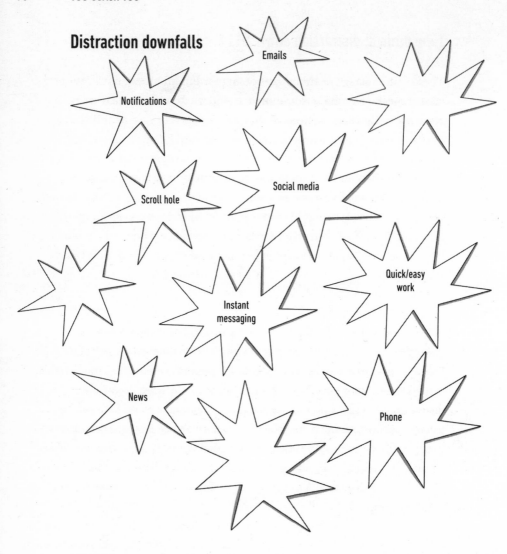

CY? What is my biggest distraction downfall?

_____

CY? How does it get in my way?

_____

CY? What are the benefits of overcoming my distraction downfall?

_____

Now we want to consider how you can add friction to your distractions to make them less appealing and harder to access. For example, you could turn off notifications, leave your phone in a different room or logout of your email while you're working on a project so you're less tempted to have a quick look at what's happening elsewhere.

CY? How could I add friction to my distraction to make it less appealing and harder to access?

PART 2: Your work–life fit

So far in this chapter you have increased your awareness of how you spend your time today and identified actions related to both *what* you spend time on and *how effective* your return on time invested is. In this section we focus on how you can approach your work–life fit. Before we share some exercises, the list below sets the scene for the mindset shift we need to make away from unrealistic expectations of balance to a more realistic and useful perspective on the role that work plays in our lives today.

From: Work–life balance		To: Work–life fit
Perfect balance	→	Imperfect fit
Having it all	→	What's most important right now
I should be doing	→	I'm doing my best
For women	→	For everyone

Your Netflix work–life documentary

This is a fun way to reflect on the headlines of what's happening in your life at the moment and how that's changed over time. Imagine that since starting your career you have been followed by a camera crew from Netflix making a documentary series. Think about:

- How many different series have you had so far?
- How would you sum up each series in one word?
- What are the headlines for each series?
- What's the 'teaser' for the next series? (As a viewer, what do I have to look forward to?)
- How would you describe your work–life fit?

We've included an example for Sarah below.

Series 1: 'Pretending'
Headlines: Wore a lot of black, pretended to be an extrovert, played a lot of netball.
Work–life fit: very low / low / average / (good) / very good / brilliant

Series 2: 'Intense'
Headlines: Moved to London, worked lots and loved it, started side projects, volunteered, full-on.
Work–life fit: very low / low / average/ good / very good / (brilliant)

Series 3: (current series): 'Brave'
Headlines: Redundancy, starting a family (hard time) and a business (right before Covid) with the best person (Helen).
Work–life fit: very low / low / (average) / good / very good / brilliant

Series 4 (coming soon): 'Growing'
Headlines: Growing and looking after my family and my business.
Work–life fit: very low / low / average/ (good) / very good / brilliant.

You can use the template opposite to create your own work–life documentary.

My work–life documentary

Series 1: _____

Headlines: _____

_____

Work–life fit: very low / low
                       / average / good
                       / very good / brilliant

Series 2: _____

Headlines: _____

_____

Work–life fit: very low / low
                       / average / good
                       / very good / brilliant

Series 3: _____

Headlines: _____

_____

Work–life fit: very low / low
                       / average / good
                       / very good / brilliant

Now use your documentary reflections to answer the following coach yourself questions.

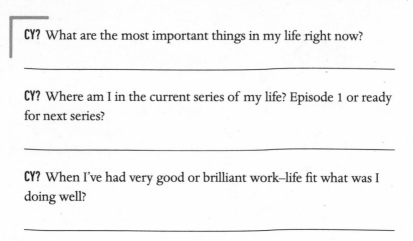

CY? What are the most important things in my life right now?

_____

CY? Where am I in the current series of my life? Episode 1 or ready for next series?

_____

CY? When I've had very good or brilliant work–life fit what was I doing well?

_____

We hope creating your work–life documentary has supported you to see the big picture and has shown how your fit changes over time and is always in flux.

By now you will have a sense of where your work–life fit is at the moment and next we're going to explore how you can improve that fit today, this week and every week.

Fitting together the pieces of your puzzle

We all have different pieces of our individual puzzle that we're trying to fit together in a way that works for us. Take five minutes to reflect on what your puzzle pieces are and make a note of them in the diagram opposite (there are some examples underneath the diagram).

My puzzle pieces

Examples: kids, work, exercise, friends, partner, family, hobbies, learning, personal projects

Rather than trying to keep all your puzzle pieces constantly fitted together, we'd suggest trying a different approach where you prioritize fitting together the pieces that are most important for you right now.

Consider each of the following coach yourself questions:

CY? Which pieces of my puzzle need to fit together today?

_____

CY? How would I like my puzzle to fit together this week?

_____

CY? Which piece of my puzzle never seems to find a place to fit?

_____

CY? What are my options for my puzzle piece that doesn't fit?

_____

We describe this continual rearranging of your puzzle pieces as 'constant calibration'. It's something we both do all the time. Every week we ask each other the same two questions over WhatsApp and reply with a thumbs up or thumbs down:

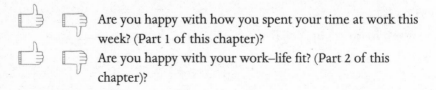   Are you happy with how you spent your time at work this week? (Part 1 of this chapter)?

Are you happy with your work–life fit? (Part 2 of this chapter)?

This simple and quick check-in gives us immediate feedback on how we're both doing. If either of us responds with a thumbs down it prompts us to ask ourselves the following coach yourself questions:

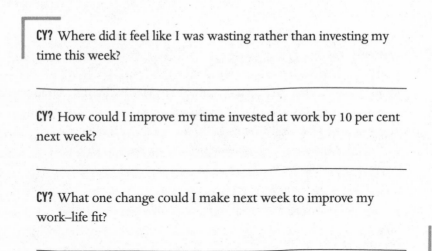

CY? Where did it feel like I was wasting rather than investing my time this week?

_____

CY? How could I improve my time invested at work by 10 per cent next week?

_____

CY? What one change could I make next week to improve my work–life fit?

_____

Work–life conflict

As you begin fitting the pieces of your puzzle together you might identify influences on your fit that seem out of your control. These probably feel like the biggest barriers to improving your fit. Perhaps it's your manager's expectations about how you work, a relocation of your office that increases your commute, an urgent and 'must do' project that comes your way or your partner's change of job affects your childcare. While we can't control outside influences, we can coach ourselves to identify the conflict they create for us and the immediate and medium-term choices available to us.

CY? What influences, that feel out of my control, are negatively impacting my work–life fit right now?

1. _____

2. _____

3. _____

For each of these influences, reflect on what conflict that creates for you. For example, in one of Sarah's roles she was relocated to an office further from home. Her (often unpredictable) commute increased to two hours a day and she also needed to drop off and pick up her toddler from nursery. The commute and the toddler were two immovable items that didn't fit together, making life, and Sarah, very stressed. For Helen, a new and challenging manager introduced a significant amount of conflict into her life. Her manager had a very different style from her own and Helen felt unable to lead her team and manage her work in a way that was authentic to her. Over time she began to feel frustrated and demotivated in her role. At their worst, these moments of conflict leave us feeling helpless and unhappy. But once we accept the conflict as our reality (as much as we might not like it) we can move on to uncovering the choices we have. For Sarah and her unsustainable commute this meant considering whether she could work in a different way (hours or location or even a new role) and talking to her manager, partner and support network about how they could help her. And for Helen, with the manager mismatch, her choices included talking to colleagues about their experience and approach, giving feedback to the manager and exploring new roles.

Considering choices helps you feel that you can move through a situation rather than staying stuck.

You can use the following coach yourself questions to generate your choices:

CY? What would a good, better and best outcome look like for me?

Good _____

Better _____

Best _____

CY? Who could I learn from who has experienced similar conflict to me before?

_____

CY? What compromises or changes would I be willing to make in order to move forward?

_____

Ten time tactics

For the final section of this chapter we've shared ten different tactics to help you manage your time at work. These are not the 'answers' but techniques you can experiment with to see what works for you. Sarah finds 'to-think lists' very helpful whereas Helen is a big fan of the two-minute rule.

1. Monk mode

This is the act of focusing on one specific task and shutting off all other distractions. It's a commitment to yourself to get your work done and requires you to eliminate any time-wasting activities that might get in your way. Monk mode is a great tactic when you want to think more deeply or you're up against a deadline. Try to create a two-hour window in your diary to work on something you are passionate about but might have been putting off. Remove all distractions from your room and see how far you can get.

2. Pomodoro technique

This technique allows you to break down big projects into doable chunks of work. Each chunk of work is called a 'pomodoro' and lasts for twenty-five minutes. Each pomodoro is followed by a short break of five minutes and the intention is to complete four pomodoros before having a longer thirty-minute break. This technique, developed by Francesco Cirillo in the late 1980s using a tomato-shaped timer (hence 'pomodoro'!), has been shown to help people focus and build momentum. You can download a pomodoro app like Focus Booster or Tomatoes and set yourself a challenge of doing a full cycle of pomodoros to make progress on a work project.

3. To-think lists

To-do lists are helpful for keeping a log of jobs to be done, but they are very task focused. A to-think list reminds you of the areas you want to reflect on and unsolved problems and challenges you want to think through. These areas that need your brain power

are often forgotten or under-appreciated in our day-to-day focus on getting stuff done. At the start of each week try writing a to-think list alongside your to-do list and work out when you're going to make time for your thinking.

4. Goalden hour

We all have times of the day when we are more productive than others. Perhaps you're an early bird or maybe you produce your best work at night. The goalden hour is about playing to our natural productivity strengths and doing our most creative and important work during that time. This will help you to make consistent progress towards the goals that matter most to you. Keep a diary for a week that tracks when you feel most energized and alert. Use this to identify your goalden hour and block it out in your diary for your highest quality work.

5. Productivity partner

We find it easier to stick to our plans when someone holds us to account. Having a productivity partner means letting someone know what you want to achieve and by when. Sometimes this can mean working side-by-side with the person or it can just be someone who texts you at the end of the day to see how you're getting on. Productivity partners should feel like a supportive presence rather than a critical one. If you're stuck with finding someone you could try using Focusmate (focusmate.com), which is a virtual co-working site that pairs you up with someone to work with. You connect via video conference, start by sharing your respective goals and then work in tandem for fifty minutes at a time.

6. Music mindset

Music has been shown to help increase our focus and flow. Studies show that 90 per cent of people perform better when listening to music, and 88 per cent of employees produce more accurate work when listening to music.[21] Music can also help to manage stress at work as it stimulates dopamine in our brains, which makes us feel happier. Create your own productivity playlist with the music that helps you to focus and find some space in your day to go into your music mindset. You can also search for ready-made mindset playlists on Spotify and YouTube.

7. Two-minute rule

David Allen is famous for 'Getting Things Done' (GTD), a time management system that has a huge following and was described by Wired in 2005 as a 'new cult for the info age'. One feature of GTD is the two-minute rule, the idea that tasks that can be completed in under two minutes should be done and dusted and not put off for another day. These two-minute tasks don't even make it onto your to-do list, they just get done, preventing bottlenecks. The best approach to two-minute tasks is to do as many of them as you can in a single time slot (as you don't want them to disrupt your day). Try allocating ten minutes of your day for these tasks – this means you will get five done a day.

8. Swallow the frog

Swallowing the frog means doing our most mentally taxing work first, when we have the energy needed to tackle it. Write down three 'frogs' that you have to work on at the moment and create a 'swallow the frog' slot in your diary next week to work on the biggest one first.

9. Time blocking (and its cousins task batching and day theming)

Time blocking is setting aside specific chunks of time for activities so that you're not making lots of choices throughout a day about what to spend your time on next. This reduces context switches and encourages focus and concentration. You can take this a step further by using your time blocks for specific tasks, so in addition to blocking out 9–11 a.m. for individual work you allocate a specific task such as writing client presentations. You could even choose to theme one or two of your days in a week, for example Mondays and Tuesdays might be your team and meeting days, whereas Fridays might be for creative work.

10. Time-saving templates

We can often find ourselves creating the same slides from scratch or sharing similar updates via email. These repetitive tasks can be made much more efficient when we create templates that we can reuse to speed up our response. This might look like a slide deck that is preformatted or an email that already has the key bits of information in and just needs personalizing before you press send. Any time you find yourself being asked for the same information repeatedly, treat it as a signal that a time-saving template could be a helpful thing to create.

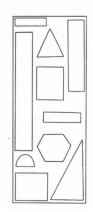

Beyond time management

The time is always right to do what is right.

MARTIN LUTHER KING JR

If you've coached yourself through this chapter, taken as many actions as you can and still feel frustrated with how you are spending your time and your work–life fit, perhaps time is not really the problem. Maybe you're in a job that requires you to work in a way that doesn't suit your style of working at your best. Perhaps your organization's culture is working against rather than for you. If this resonates, we suggest coaching yourself through purpose (Chapter 7) and progression (Chapter 6) next. These chapters will help you think about what matters most to you and how you align that to the work you do. The insights and ideas from this chapter won't go to waste as even small changes can help you to feel more in control in the short term.

Ask our expert: Graham Allcott, author and podcast host of *Beyond Busy*

Productivity is more about what you say no to than what you say yes to. And if your no's never feel uncomfortable or like there's a trade-off, you're not saying no often enough.

Coaching question: *I can't get things done because my days are dominated by meetings. I can't see how I can escape the meeting overload and I feel really frustrated that I'm not making progress on work that matters to me. What can I do to become more productive?*

Expert answer: Many people and organizations resort to 'let's set up a meeting' because in truth it's easier than 'let's make a decision'. You want to avoid any meeting that is a substitute for someone else's clearer thinking. But it's also about balance: great meetings change the world, and sometimes a meeting together can be greater than the sum of the parts. I talk about this as the 'Yin and Yang of meetings'. Yin is about collaboration, and meetings offer a space to generously share attention with each other, to reflect, learn and listen. Meetings like this are vital to keep a team in tune with each other and help fix the little things that start to fail in isolation.

But we also need Yang. Creation. Action. Being heads-down doing the 'real work'. It sounds from your question like you're desperately craving some Yang to 'actually get some work done', so I'll focus on that here, with five solutions for you to mix and match, depending on the culture and situation:

1. **The collective solution:** If you're in a position to influence the culture, set everyone the 'take five' challenge: each person has to save five hours of the organization's time by deleting existing meetings (so a one-hour meeting with five people = five working hours). Ask everyone to bring their solutions to your next team meeting, and use this to facilitate a discussion about meeting less.

2. **The role model solution:** In every meeting you organize, include a purpose statement (e.g. 'by the end of the meeting we will have . . .'), an agenda (with timings) and a summary of your reasons for inviting each attendee ('Helen, we really need your marketing brain on items 3, 4 and 5 of the agenda', and so on). All this is observed by colleagues and encourages them to do the same. Brevity comes from clarity.

3. **The 'gentle pushback' solution:** If you can't say no, your rule should be 'no agenda, no meeting'. Why should you commit before you know what it actually is? The best practice version here is 'no purpose statement, no meeting'. This helps clarify if you're actually needed. You can also ask if it's OK for you to make a cameo (in Helen's case above, 'I'm pushed for time this week, would you mind if I just popped in for the relevant marketing agenda items?').

4. **The stealth solution:** Make it harder to book time in your calendar for a meeting. Have rules. Mine is that I write during the morning and meet during the afternoon. Yours may be less extreme, but the point is to align your calendar with your intentions. Simple, but often neglected. If you don't think your colleagues would respect seeing things like 'heads-down work time' in your diary, then change it to something stealthy like 'Project Magenta'. It sounds intriguing, confidential and important. They'll leave you alone and work around it.

5. **The naughty schoolboy solution:** A lot of us have those regular meetings we're politically obliged to attend but don't feel like we're adding much value. If you're not in a position to question the status quo, then set a secret 'attend one in three' kind of policy for yourself – 'keep your toe in' but reclaim some time.

   Productivity is more about what you say no to than what you say yes to. And if your no's never feel uncomfortable or like there's a trade-off, you're not saying no often enough.

You COACH You

You can use the COACH tool to bring together your thoughts and reflections from this chapter and apply them to the specific career challenge you might be facing at the moment. Taking the time to bring your insights together using COACH will help you to be clear about your actions, increase your confidence and spot the support you need. The more you practise using COACH, the more you'll find yourself using it for lots of different challenges both at work and in your career.

COACH

Clarity – what is your coaching challenge?

Options – what options could you explore?

Action – what actions will you take?

Confidence – how confident are you about taking those actions?

Help – what help do you need to overcome your challenge?

Summary

Time: How you take control of your time at work.

All we have to decide is what to do with the time that is given us.
J. R. R. Tolkien

Why coach yourself?	Coach yourself concepts
To move beyond busy and increase the quality of the work that you do.	**Task:time ratio:** How you know whether you're spending time on the work that matters most.
To take control of the role that work plays in your life and find your own work–life fit.	**Distraction downfalls:** The things that get in the way of spending your time well.
	Work–life fit: How you can fit together the most important parts of your life this week.

COACHING TOOLS

Time trade-offs

IF I want to increase my time on...

THEN I need to decrease my time on...

Managing your monkeys

My monkeys = my priorities

Other people's monkeys = distraction

Work–life fit

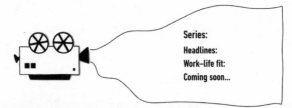

Series:
Headlines:
Work–life fit:
Coming soon...

COACH YOURSELF QUESTIONS
1. How in control of my time do I feel?
2. What would I most like to change about how I spend my time at work?
3. When do I feel present, immersed and absorbed in my work?
4. What gets in the way of doing my best work?
5. What does a week well spent look like for me?

Listen	Free downloads
Squiggly Careers podcast #238 with Oliver Burkeman	www.amazingif.com

Time you enjoyed wasting, was not wasted.

JOHN LENNON

Always remember
you are braver
than you believe,
stronger than
you seem, and
smarter than
you think.

CHRISTOPHER
ROBIN

4 → Self-belief

How you build the beliefs that help you succeed

Self-belief: why coach yourself?

1. Everyone experiences self-doubt and it can lead to a sense of not being 'enough' in some way at work. When we understand, rather than avoid, our doubts we can better respond to negative emotions and stop a lack of self-belief from holding us back.
2. We are continually coping with change and learning new skills to stay up to date. Uncertainty can feel uncomfortable, and while we can't control what happens around us, we can take control of building positive beliefs that help us to be successful at work.

Self-doubt is data

Everybody experiences self-doubt, it's how our brains protect us from potential pitfalls and problems. Avoiding or denying these doubts doesn't help us, it only amplifies them further.[22] Psychologist Susan David recommends that instead of ignoring our doubts we can use them as data, and by recognizing and acknowledging our emotions

> I have written eleven books, but each time I think, 'Uh-oh, they're going to find out now. I've run a game on everybody, and they're going to find me out'.
>
> **MAYA ANGELOU**

we put ourselves in a better position to understand how our fears might be holding us back. David suggests we should see our doubts *as flashing lights to the things we care about* and her research has shown that something called 'emotional agility' helps us to move from self-doubt to self-belief. Emotional agility means we recognize our emotions and choose to react and respond in a way that builds our belief, rather than letting doubt drive our actions.

The comparison curse

Career comparison is common and contributes to our sense of not being enough. A poll by Bumble Bizz showed that 86 per cent of people compare their career paths to those of others. Career comparison creeps in when we judge how much we earn, how 'successful' we are and how big an impact we make based on what we observe in the people around us. A study by economist Angus Deaton and psychologist Daniel Kahneman in 2010 found that it's how our income compares with our friends' rather than how much we actually earn that affects our life satisfaction. We often find ourselves unconsciously creating a scale of career success, which inevitably leads to self-doubt as there will always be people 'ahead' of us.

> *Always be a first-rate version of yourself and not a second-rate version of someone else.*
>
> **JUDY GARLAND**

What are beliefs?

Beliefs are how we make sense of the world and act as energy-saving shortcuts for our brain.[23] We use them to predict what will happen and understand how things relate to each other. Creating a new belief or challenging an existing one is difficult. Our default when we receive new

> *Belief is a mental architecture of how we interpret the world.*
>
> **PETER HALLIGAN**

information is to find a way to fit what we learn into the existing belief framework we have in our minds. For example, if you have a negative belief that sounds like *I'm not smart enough*, when you are unsuccessful in a job application your inner voice might tell you *I knew I wasn't clever enough for that job and this proves my point*. Alternatively, if you have a positive belief that sounds like *I'm always learning and improving*, you respond to an unsuccessful job application by asking yourself *How could I get better for next time?* Our beliefs can work for or against us, and we all have both positive and negative beliefs about ourselves.

Self-belief is a skill

Self-belief is a skill, it's not something that is fixed, and we all have the ability to learn how to build our own belief. You can't 'see' self-belief, but you can spot evidence it exists in our actions and behaviours. It looks like making ambitious and brave choices in your career. It looks like responding positively to moments of doubt when things don't go to plan. It

> *You will only achieve what you tell yourself you can do. Let yourself believe that there may be more.*
>
> **LUCY GOSSAGE**

looks like achieving our goals. Self-belief shows up in small ways too: the confidence to say no to an unrealistic deadline or offering a different point of view to your manager or supporting a colleague to challenge the status quo.

Sources of self-belief

Psychologist Albert Bandura was one of the pioneers of research to progress our understanding of self-belief. Bandura found that, though some of our belief is built in childhood, we continue to evolve our beliefs throughout our lives. He identified four significant sources of self-efficacy (a person's belief in their ability to succeed in a particular situation):

1. **Mastery:** doing something successfully builds our belief.
2. **Modelling:** seeing people similar to us succeed helps us to believe we can do it too.

3. Encouragement: people believing in you and giving you positive feedback.
4. Difficulty: responding to challenging situations and tasks with optimism rather than stress.

Bandura found that people with a strong sense of self-belief are more interested in and committed to their activities and recover quickly from setbacks. For these people difficulty and failure don't mean defeat; instead they increase their efforts and look for new ways to overcome challenges.

> *Self-belief means seeing yourself, and your situation, clearly and compassionately.*

Self-belief does not mean responding to mistakes at work or the 'downs' in our career by being relentlessly or unrealistically positive about ourselves, and it doesn't guarantee a straight line to success (listen to Elizabeth Day interviewing her very 'successful' guests on her excellent *How to Fail* podcast to see this is true). Research by Heidi Grant has shown that people who respond to their own shortcomings with self-compassion are the most likely to improve their performance.[24] Self-compassion is a willingness to look at your failures with kindness and understanding. When you make a mistake or things don't go to plan you can view the situation with awareness and objectivity. You don't judge yourself harshly (as you recognize that no one is perfect) or get defensive and feel the need to remind people of your successes (letting go of your ego). This doesn't mean letting yourself off the hook, it's about seeing a situation clearly and challenging yourself to continually improve and look for ways to be even better. Serena Chen has found that self-compassion not only improves our performance, but also increases our optimism and general well-being.[25]

> *Even the most 'successful' people experience self-doubt.*

Before we move on to thinking traps and positive prompts, here is a short story from the sporting world to show what's possible personally and professionally when we take control of our self-belief. On the podcast *Life Lessons: From Sport and Beyond*, cancer doctor and triathlete Lucy Gossage describes herself as a rational and logical person with irrational thoughts about herself. Her self-doubt even led to slowing down in races to allow other people, whom she considered to be 'better', to overtake her. She shares how, after some gentle nudging from a sports psychologist friend, she started to work on her self-talk and prepare her brain with the same rigour as she prepares her body. This positively impacted all areas of her life, not only in winning races (she has been an Ironman champion fourteen times) but also in giving her the confidence to reduce her workload as a doctor to a part-time basis, so she has capacity for her charity work and personal passions.

Thinking traps and positive prompts

Thinking traps are a useful way to identify any assumptions you have that could get in the way of being open and optimistic in your coaching approach.

   I'm worried that if I improve my self-belief I'll be perceived as arrogant.
   Self-belief doesn't feel like something I can learn.
   I'll only build belief by being successful.
   I'm too set in my ways to challenge my beliefs.
   It doesn't matter how much I build my belief, things never seem to go my way at work.

Reframing your thinking traps as positive prompts will unlock your assumptions and give you the ability to explore options and possibilities as you coach yourself.

From: I'm worried that if I improve my self-belief I'll be perceived as arrogant.
To: How would I describe other people I admire who have strong self-belief?

From: Self-belief doesn't feel like something I can learn.
To: What has helped me to feel confident in the past?

From: I'll only build belief by being successful.
To: What have I learnt from the mistakes I've made at work?

From: I'm too set in my ways to challenge my beliefs.
To: What could some of the benefits of challenging my negative beliefs be?

From: It doesn't matter how much I build my belief, things never seem to go my way at work.
To: What three things am I most proud of at work in the past twelve months?

My self-belief thinking trap

_____

My self-belief positive prompt

_____

How to build your self-belief

The next section of the chapter will show you how you can build your self-belief. We will support you to coach yourself on both how you can build your belief every day and how to respond if you're experiencing a setback.

In Part 1 we'll cover:

~ *How to understand your current levels of self-belief based on what you think, say and do.*

⤿ *How to take actions that will build your belief including changing from a limiting to limitless lens, saying no and spending more time in your courage zone.*

In Part 2 we focus on:

⤿ *How setback stories and our seven setback coach yourself questions are useful techniques to work through for every career challenge.*
⤿ *How to coach yourself if you're experiencing a common career setback: redundancy, out of your depth, critical feedback and when things don't go to plan.*

The chapter ends with advice from two experts. Eleanor Tweddell, author of *Why Losing Your Job Could be the Best Thing That Ever Happened to You*, offers practical ideas and actions for anyone experiencing redundancy and Elizabeth Uviebinené, author of *Slay in your Lane* and *Reset*, who shares her words of wisdom on how to overcome imposter syndrome.

PART 1: Building blocks of self-belief

It can be hard to know how to get started with improving your self-belief as it's a big topic with lots of different dimensions. We have designed the next exercise so you can understand where you already have positive beliefs and identify the areas of self-doubt that you want to work on. We think of this as a wall of self-belief: the more bricks you have in place, the stronger your belief will be.

You can improve your awareness of how strong your self-belief is today by reflecting on what you *think*, *say* and *do* at work.

Step 1: Answer each of the nine questions below by circling either the A or the B statement, depending on what feels most true for you.

Step 2: For every A answer, shade in the corresponding numbered brick on your wall of belief. Leave those bricks where you circled B statements unshaded.

Your building blocks of self-belief

Question 1

A: You think that you have the abilities to do your job well.

B: You often think that you're not enough in some way.

Question 2

A: You make your own mind up about what you think about yourself.

B: You worry about what other people's opinions of you are.

Question 3

A: You think about your strengths and how you can make them stronger.

B: You think about your weaknesses and the mistakes that you have made.

Question 4

A: You say I can more than I can't.

B: You say I can't more than I can.

Question 5

A: You say thank you to praise and feel good about the difference you make.

B: You dismiss compliments as untrue or just people being nice.

Question 6

A: You say no when you need to.

B: You say yes when you would like to say no.

Question 7

A: You spend time with people who boost your belief.

B: You spend time with people who make you feel worse about yourself.

Question 8

A: You share and celebrate your successes.

B: You find it hard to know the impact you make in your job.

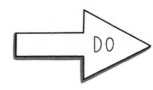

Question 9

A: You spend some of your time doing tasks you've never done before.

B: You spend most of your time doing tasks you're comfortable with.

Your wall of belief

DOING	7		8		9	
SAYING		4		5		6
THINKING	1		2		3	

You now have a wall with a mixture of shaded and unshaded bricks. The shaded bricks are where you already have positive beliefs about yourself. You will continue to work on building these beliefs, but you have good foundations in place to start from. The unshaded bricks are where your negative beliefs might be holding you back, these are the areas we suggest you prioritize.

Before we move on to action, take a couple of minutes to reflect on the following three coach yourself questions.

CY? What trends or themes can I spot across my building blocks of belief (for example, do you have most of your gaps in the thinking, saying or doing area)?

_____

CY? What am I already doing well that has helped me to build my belief?

_____

CY? Which gaps in my building blocks feel like the biggest barriers to my self-belief?

_____

No one has a perfect wall of self-belief and yours will change over time. Self-belief is something we need to invest in continually so that we can be our best at work.

Turns out believing in yourself is something you have to do over and over again. Cool.

ASHLEY C. FORD

What you think, you become.

SIDDHARTHA
GAUTAMA
(THE BUDDHA)

In the next section, we will help you to coach yourself to take positive action to build your belief across each of the thinking, saying and doing areas.

Think

As we mentioned in the introduction to this chapter, it's not easy to change, challenge or reconstruct our beliefs. When we form a negative belief about ourselves at work, whether it's true or not, it sticks with us. These beliefs limit us in lots of ways. We limit our learning, our options, our curiosity, our adaptability and our willingness to experiment. These are all behaviours we need in order to make the most of our careers and without them we are vulnerable to change. Rationally we usually recognize these beliefs hold us back, but they are so deep-seated that it can feel both difficult and daunting to do anything differently.

Your limiting lens

Limiting lenses affect our perception of the world around us. They distort reality and lead to negative thoughts about what we can and can't do. Have a look at the different examples of limiting lenses opposite. Do any of these feel familiar for you? Each limiting lens creates a set of negative beliefs and we've shared some examples of how each lens might impact your thoughts and how it could hold you back.

Limiting lenses		
Limiting lens	**What you might think**	**How it might hold you back**
Black and white	*If I don't succeed in the way I set out to I'm a failure.*	Over time you reduce your ambitions and go for goals that feel safe.
Catastrophizing	*Everything is going wrong at work. It's a complete disaster.*	You magnify mistakes and focus on problems rather than spotting solutions.
Fixing my future	*It didn't work out for me before so there's no point trying again.*	You stop exploring opportunities to progress.
I'm not enough	*I'm not as good as my colleagues and I'm going to get found out.*	You don't proactively share your opinion or ask questions and you reduce your impact.

My limiting lens

The limiting lens that I wear most frequently is:

Using the exercise above, now reflect on the following coach yourself questions:

CY? What do the negative thoughts I have about myself at work sound like (e.g. I've not got enough experience to progress)?

_____

CY? When have my negative thoughts held me back at work (e.g. not applying for jobs I'm interested in)?

_____

Limiting to limitless lens

To challenge our thinking, we need to change the lens through which we're viewing our own world. When we change the lens we're wearing, we change our beliefs about who we are and what we can achieve. By trying on a new limitless lens, we challenge our current status quo and start to see the world in a new way. We change our negative beliefs to positive beliefs, and you can see how this works in the table below.

Limiting to limitless lens		
From: Limiting lens	**To: Limitless lens**	**How it moves you forward**
Black and white	*Shades of grey*	You are able to explore alternative options if your initial plans don't progress in the way you had hoped.
Catastrophizing	*Seeing solutions*	You recognize that everyone makes mistakes and that it's natural to feel disappointed but know the most important thing is to learn and move forward.
Fixing my future	*Flexible futures*	You regularly have curious career conversations to explore areas of interest, build your career community and increase the breadth of your progression possibilities.
I'm not enough	*I am enough*	You volunteer for new projects you're interested in as you are confident about your strengths and the value you can add.
My limitless lens		
The limitless lens I'm going to try on is:		

Changing our beliefs

When you change from a limiting to a limitless lens you can start to change the beliefs you hold about yourself. You can coach yourself to spot and stop the negative beliefs you find yourself thinking and create a more positive belief. We've shared some examples of common negative beliefs below and how they become positive if you change the lens you're wearing. We've then left a couple of blank thought bubbles for you to add in your own reflections.

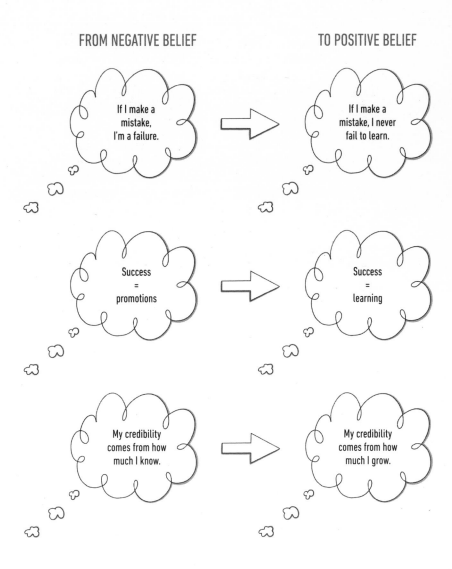

FROM NEGATIVE BELIEF   TO POSITIVE BELIEF

If I make a mistake, I'm a failure.

If I make a mistake, I never fail to learn.

Success = promotions

Success = learning

My credibility comes from how much I know.

My credibility comes from how much I grow.

MY NEGATIVE BELIEFS   MY POSITIVE BELIEFS

You can now use the diagram below to bring together your insights from the previous exercises. This simple snapshot is a useful tool to keep coming back to whenever you're grappling with negative thoughts and beliefs about yourself.

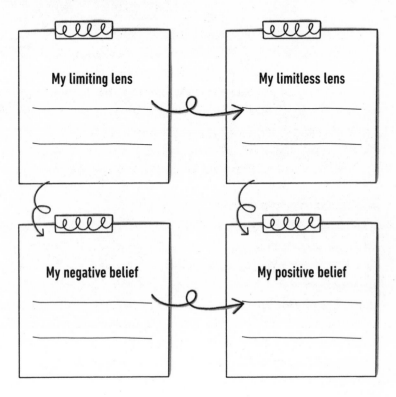

Say

Self-talk

> Don't be a VICTIM of
> negative self-talk –
> remember YOU are
> listening.
>
> **BOB PROCTOR**

We all have an inner voice that keeps us company as
we go through our days. This inner voice, or self-talk,
combines conscious and unconscious thoughts, beliefs and biases
that we have, and provides a way for our brain to interpret and process our
experiences. In his excellent book *Chatter*, Ethan Kross vividly describes
our inner voice as both a 'helpful superpower and destructive kryptonite
that hurts us'. This is the difference between the inner coach and inner
critic concept that we described in Chapter 1, 'How to Coach Yourself'.

Idea for action: first-person vs fly-on-the-wall

This coaching technique helps you to gain perspective on a challenge in an
objective way. Distance changes our self-talk, which, as Kross points out,
'doesn't solve our problems, but it increases the likelihood that we can. It
unclouds our verbal stream.' The next time you experience a tough time
during the work week take five minutes to view your situation in the first
person and then as a fly on the wall to see what impact it has on your
levels of self-belief. We've shared an example of how this can work in
practice and left space for you to try this out for yourself.

Example

Experience/situation where you feel your inner critic creeping in:
In a meeting my manager didn't agree with my proposal for a new project.

First-person self-talk:
*This is all my fault, I'm so frustrated with myself, I'm not smart enough to be
    doing this job, I'm a failure.*

Fly-on-the-wall self-talk:
*In the team meeting Sarah's manager agreed with her ideas but felt this wasn't
    the right time to pursue the project given other team priorities. Other
    team members also shared their support for Sarah's ideas, and they were
    particularly interested in concept A.*

First-person vs fly-on-the-wall self-talk

Describe a recent experience at work where your inner critic took over:

_____

First-person self-talk sounds like:

_____

Fly-on-the-wall self-talk sounds like:

_____

Idea for action: say your name, say your name

Using your own name when you're talking to yourself has been shown to be a quick and easy way to move from self-doubt to self-belief. It helps us to approach stressful situations as challenges, putting our growth mindset of 'can' in control rather than feeling fixed and 'can't'. Another belief-building approach to self-talk is an even smaller shift: from saying 'I' to saying 'you' instead. Kross found in his research that when we talk to ourselves using 'you' it generates a significant improvement in our ability to learn from and process negative emotions and experiences rather than only reliving them. An example of each of these techniques is in the table below to show how this works in practice.

	Self-doubt	Self-belief
Saying your own name	*This is a challenging opportunity – I'm not sure I can do this.*	*Helen, this is an exciting opportunity – you can do it.*
Using 'you' rather than 'I'	*I didn't do a good job in that presentation, I keep thinking about all the mistakes that I made.*	*You can learn a lot when things don't go to plan. For example, you can see why it's important to not share too much data at once as it can be overwhelming for people listening.*

To practise shifting your self-talk to build your belief, answer the three coach yourself questions below.

CY? What feels stressful at work for me right now?

Example: too many projects and not enough time.

_____

CY? What does the negative self-talk in my head sound like?

Example: I worry that I'm not doing a very good job of any of them.

_____

CY? How would this self-talk be different if I used my name and 'you' rather than 'I'?

Example: Helen, you have managed multiple projects before and you can do it again. You love your work, and that passion will show up in what you do. Keep going . . .

_____

Saying no

Most of us are hardwired to be helpful, which makes saying no hard. In the situations where we say yes, but would like to say no, our behaviour is typically being driven by a fear of some sort. The fear that our manager will think that we can't cope, the fear that someone will think we're not good at our job, the fear of what someone will say about us. However, saying no helps to build our belief in two important ways:

> It is only by saying no that you can concentrate on the things that are really important.
>
> **STEVE JOBS**

1. Saying no to some things means we can say yes to more opportunities to use our strengths, which in turn boosts our belief and increases our chances of success.
2. Saying no reduces our stress and risk of burnout, which then means we have more capacity to approach challenges with optimism and a can-do attitude.

Before we explore some practical ideas for action on how to say no, consider the following coach yourself questions:

CY? When have I wanted to say no but said yes instead?

_____

CY? Why did I say yes, when I wanted to say no?

_____

CY? When do I feel confident saying no to people?

_____

CY? What has helped me to say no in the past?

_____

Idea for action: your need to say no

To start practising saying no when you need to it's useful to have some go-to responses that you feel comfortable saying and can start trying out. See if any of the yes/no scenarios below feel familiar to you and use the yes/no responses to identify what the implications of saying yes versus no could be for you.

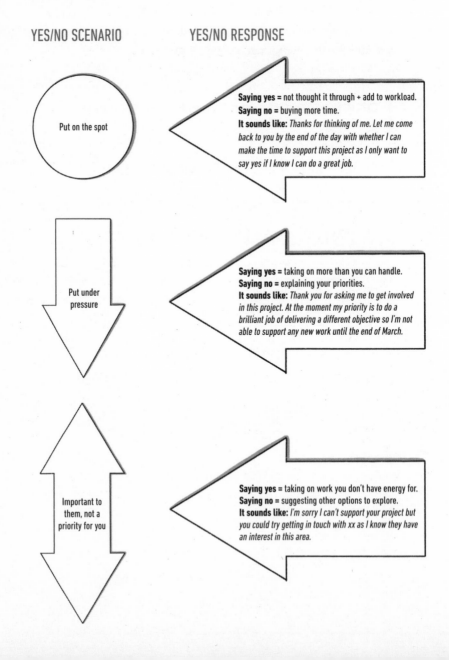

YES/NO SCENARIO

YES/NO RESPONSE

Put on the spot

Saying yes = not thought it through + add to workload.
Saying no = buying more time.
It sounds like: *Thanks for thinking of me. Let me come back to you by the end of the day with whether I can make the time to support this project as I only want to say yes if I know I can do a great job.*

Put under pressure

Saying yes = taking on more than you can handle.
Saying no = explaining your priorities.
It sounds like: *Thank you for asking me to get involved in this project. At the moment my priority is to do a brilliant job of delivering a different objective so I'm not able to support any new work until the end of March.*

Important to them, not a priority for you

Saying yes = taking on work you don't have energy for.
Saying no = suggesting other options to explore.
It sounds like: *I'm sorry I can't support your project but you could try getting in touch with xx as I know they have an interest in this area.*

Do

Creating your courage zone

> It is your right to choose what you do and don't do, to choose what you believe in and don't believe in. It is your right to curate your life and your own perspective.
>
> **LADY GAGA**

Your comfort zone is when work feels familiar and 'safe'. This usually means you can make quick and efficient progress and at the same time recover your energy for harder work. Spending time in your comfort zone is not a bad thing, but too much time spent here means we risk staying still rather than stretching ourselves. Your courage zone is when work feels daunting and even 'scary' in some way. If you approach creating your courage zone in the right way it will build your belief, as you will test your assumptions about your abilities and discover you can do more than you give yourself credit for by exploring your potential.

My comfort vs courage zone

The doughnut diagram below represents your working week. Shade in the percentage of time you currently spend in your courage zone in an average week.

Example: 20% time in my courage zone

Time in my courage zone

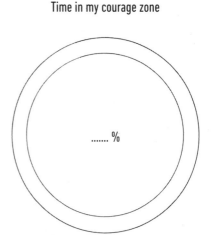

.... %

Scary scenarios

Your comfort and courage zones are personal to you and look and feel different for each of us. To spend more time in your courage zone you need to be specific about what that looks like for you. Start by writing down three 'scary scenarios' for you at work. These scenarios are tasks that you feel you can't do or that are out of reach in some way.

My scary scenarios

1. _____
2. _____
3. _____

For each scary scenario, write down the fears you have about the task that is driving your self-doubt. You might have different fears for each scenario or spot that the same fear is driving each task to feel scary.

My fear factors

1. _____
2. _____
3. _____

Our fears are typically driven by the unpredictability of the outcomes for each of the scary scenarios. In other words, a fear of the unknown and failure. Your scary scenario could be something you've tried before and felt didn't go well, or it could be a new scenario, so you don't have any data (other than your doubts) to help you figure out your chances of success. Spending more time in your courage zone means that you need to do two things: identify opportunities and say yes when you might have previously said no. When it comes to your courage zone, think of yourself more as the tortoise than the hare. You don't want to rush straight to the scariest task you can imagine as chances are that will feel too daunting or you'll stall along the way. Instead, identify a small action you can take to move into your courage zone. At this stage the most important thing is to cross the starting line, not to win the race (and remember, the tortoise wins the race eventually anyway).

Small actions to get started #bemoretortoise

For each of your scary scenarios write down one small action to get you started.

1. _____
2. _____
3. _____

Finally, sharing your scary scenarios with other people has two advantages. Saying our scenarios out loud turns them from thoughts to actions that we feel more committed to. The people we talk to can also spot opportunities on our behalf and support us along the way. To finish this exercise, write down the name of one person you could share each of your scary scenarios with and note when you intend to have that conversation, as being clear about the time and place gives us an extra nudge to make it happen.

Saying what scares us

1. Who _____ When _____
2. Who _____ When _____
3. Who _____ When _____

Idea for action: brief moments of discomfort (BMD)

This idea comes from Farrah Storr, author of *The Discomfort Zone*. Storr says that we assume spending time in our courage zone will be full of fear, but the reality is that we experience brief moments of discomfort. She says to think of it a bit like high-intensity fitness training: we experience short, sharp shocks that deliver huge gains. When we understand our BMDs we can be better prepared for them and learn how to recognize and respond to them when they happen.

A few coach yourself BMD questions to consider:

CY? What brief moments of discomfort might happen for me this week at work?

Example: I have to give a presentation in my team meeting, and I'm scared of public speaking.

_____

CY? How does a brief moment of discomfort show up in my actions?

Example: I might stutter or forget what I'm planning to say.

_____

CY? When I feel a brief moment of discomfort what could help me?

Example: Being vulnerable and sharing that you find speaking nerve racking, reminding myself that my team are on my side and knowing that in ten minutes it will all be over!

_____

PART 2: Self-belief setbacks

We're now going to focus on coaching yourself through setbacks, where self-doubt will inevitably be part of the process. We have shared one coaching tool and a series of coach yourself questions that we hope will be helpful across a range of challenging career experiences. We then finish the chapter with a 'self-belief' surgery, where we suggest some specific ideas for action related to common tough moments including feeling out of your depth, redundancy, receiving difficult feedback and when something doesn't go to plan.

Setback stories

We tell ourselves stories
in order to live.

JOAN DIDION

The stories we tell ourselves when we have a setback play an important role in either rebuilding our belief or doubling down on our doubts. Setbacks cause our self-doubts to surface, encouraging us to give up, stop trying and reduce our ambitions. As we discussed at the start of this chapter the answer is not to avoid or ignore our doubts in the hope that they'll go away but to use them as data. Stories are a useful coach yourself technique for setbacks, as they help us to both build our belief and improve our self-awareness at the same time. The benefits of expressive writing have been the focus of psychologist James W. Pennebaker's research over many years. He has found that writing about our most difficult experiences helps us to feel better, understand ourselves and, like some of the self-talk ideas we described earlier in this chapter, creates a useful distance from a reality we would rather not be in.[26] The exercise on the next page will support you to write your own setback story. We've included a real example from earlier in Sarah's career to show how this works in practice.

Title: Your title is the starting point for your story. It gives the reader a sense of what your story is about and makes us want to find out more. Your title might be short and straightforward – e.g. 'Giving up numbers' – or perhaps leave us feeling intrigued – e.g. 'Lawnmowers don't define me'.

 Protagonist: This is you. Introduce us to who you are, remembering that you are much more than your job title. For example, *I'm an introvert who loves a giant yellow Post-it note. There's always a book in my bag and an idea up my sleeve.*

 Jeopardy: No story is ever straightforward. Write a couple of sentences to describe the setback you're experiencing. This will probably be a mixture of facts and feelings. For example, *Went for a promotion and prepared my heart out (even practised my answers in front of the bathroom mirror). The interview didn't go well, especially after I was asked 'How many lawnmowers do you think there are in the UK?' – which really threw me. I didn't get the job and my current role is being made redundant in the new team structure, I really don't know what's going to happen now . . .*

 Supporting characters: Who do you turn to in your story for support and who will help to bolster your belief? Who comes to your rescue in your times of need? For example, *Becky my MBA learning buddy, Rachel my work best friend, Michele my mentor and Tom my boyfriend.*

 Crescendo: You are the hero of your own story. This is where you tell us how you're going to respond and react to your setback. At this point make sure you're wearing your limitless lens glasses and have your positive beliefs front of mind. You don't need to know all the answers or have taken lots of action to be able to write the section (you can leave your reader wanting more). For example, *This is a chance to spread my wings, maybe it's time to put those giant Post-it notes to use in a new way. I wonder where else might appreciate the strengths I have to offer and who else I could learn from. I'm going to follow my curiosity and see where I land . . .*

My setback story

Protagonist	Title	Supporting characters
Jeopardy		Crescendo

Seven setback coach yourself questions

Whatever setback you're experiencing at the moment, the following coach yourself questions (and the ideas for action in the next section) will support you to start making positive progress.

My setback: ————————————————————————————

1. CY? What am I in control of as part of my current setback?

————————————————————————————

2. CY? Who could provide me with a helpful perspective on this challenge?

————————————————————————————

3. CY? When I've experienced a setback before, what has helped me to move forward?

————————————————————————————

4. CY? What can I learn from this challenge that will be useful for my career in the future?

_____

5. CY? What successes have I had (personal or professional) at the same time as this setback?

_____

6. CY? What advice would I give to my best work friend if they were experiencing this setback?

_____

7. CY? When I reflect on this setback in a year's time, what do I want to be true about how I responded?

_____

Self-belief surgery

There are moments in our career where we all need some self-belief surgery. When something takes us by surprise and makes us doubt our abilities and impact. We notice this need for emergency self-belief support most often when people are faced with redundancy, when they are in a new situation and feel out of their depth, when they have received negative or critical feedback and when plans go off track. In the final section of this chapter, we will share some ideas for action if you are experiencing any of these situations so that you can rebuild your belief and move forward with confidence.

> *When you're out of your depth, remember you know how to swim.*

Out of your depth

We often feel out of our depth when we're spending lots of time in our courage zone and doing activities that we haven't done before, such as starting a new job or taking on more responsibility. Our 'not enoughs' can emerge in these moments. We feel overwhelmed by a challenge and start to think *this is because I'm not smart enough* or *I can't cope because I'm not experienced enough*. At these times it's useful to take actions that reassure you that it is possible to move out of the deep end, and to remind yourself that where you are today isn't where you'll always be.

Idea for action: borrowed belief

While we don't want to compare ourselves to other people, we can borrow belief from positive role models. To boost your belief when you feel overwhelmed, look for people you admire and who have been in similar situations to where you are now. This is about finding relatable people who we can 'borrow' some belief from. It could be someone in or out of your organization who has been in a similar job to you. These conversations are usually reassuring, as you realize that other people have shared experiences (rather than feeling that being out of your depth is unique to you) and they might have some helpful hints and tips that worked for them.

Idea for action: switch-off Sundays

When we're overwhelmed with work, we work longer hours in the hope of getting back in control. That might be part of a short-term solution but it's also important to recognize that when we're 'always on' it adds to our stress levels, which reduces our ability to deal with self-doubt. We have to find ways to switch off and give our brains the chance to reboot.

Try switching off your phone on Sundays for part or all of the day and see what impact it has on your Mondays. Though you might initially miss the mini dopamine hits we get from messages and emails it will be worth it in return for your ability to start the week with confidence and positivity. Generally taking time away from our devices reduces stress and improves sleep, giving you a better chance of dealing with the day-to-day doubts we all experience. If you want to 'deep-dive' into the positive impact of switching off your phone we'd recommend reading Catherine Price's short and insightful book *How to Break Up with Your Phone*.

Critical feedback

Our brains all have a bias towards negativity. This doesn't mean that we're negative people, just that we spend more time processing the mistakes that we make than we do enjoying our successes, which means it's easier to recall and remind ourselves of the difficult times in our careers. Many of us are better at describing the details of our career 'failures' than our successes. When we receive negative feedback it often feels like we've failed. It feels personal, and the building blocks of self-belief that we've carefully constructed can come crumbling down, but the good news is that we can take positive action to reinforce them.

> *Accept both compliments and criticism. It takes both sun and rain for a flower to grow.*
>
> **ANON**

Idea for action: Appreciate, Acknowledge, Assess (AAA)

When we receive hard-to-hear feedback, our initial emotions of upset or anger can get in the way of understanding what someone is trying to tell us. Taking control of your immediate reaction and how you respond to the feedback can prevent a situation spiralling into negative self-belief.

Appreciate, acknowledge and assess (AAA) is a simple way of stopping the spiral.

Appreciating means that your first response is to say thank you. It might feel hard, but it can help you to move forward. The next step is to acknowledge how you're feeling. This might sound like *I am surprised and disappointed to hear you say that.* Sometimes, depending on your response to the feedback, that's as far as you will get in your first conversation and that's OK. Your next step is to assess the feedback by gathering more insight. This might mean going back to the same person and asking some follow-up questions or speaking to another colleague to get a different perspective. By using AAA to respond to hard-to-hear feedback, you take back control of the situation.

Idea for action: get the full picture

Practising is how we improve, so one way to become more comfortable with what we describe as 'even-better-if' feedback is to ask for it. No one does everything brilliantly and if you're only hearing positive feedback from your colleagues, you're not getting the full picture and limiting your opportunities to learn. Most people don't regularly give even-better-if feedback, as we worry about how to do it in a way that doesn't hurt someone's feelings. One way to make it easier is to be specific and small in your ask. Rather than asking your colleague *Could you give me some feedback on how I could be even better at my job?* you ask *What is one way I could improve my presentations at our team meetings to make them more effective?*

Redundancy

Restructures and redundancy are always hard and nearly everyone will experience one or both of them at some point during their career. If we're not careful it's a time when our self-doubts and negative beliefs can have a field day. In these moments we can lose confidence and question our abilities, so it's useful to take some actions that remind you of your successes.

> *I have been made redundant before and it is a terrible blow; redundant is a rotten word because it makes you think you are useless.*
>
> **BILLY CONNOLLY**

Idea for action: self-supporting statements

We introduced the idea of self-supporting statements in Chapter 1. As a reminder, these are positive statements that you either write down or say to yourself out loud. They remind you to believe in your abilities and help you to start the day with positive intentions. Some examples of self-supporting statements include: *I make progress at my own pace. The only person I need to compare myself to is me. My strengths are what make me good at what I do. I grow through what I go through. I control my thoughts, they don't control me.*

Idea for action: feel-good folder

When you're experiencing restructuring or redundancy it's easy to forget all the achievements you've had in a job. Take the time to bring together all your successes from the last twelve months into one place. Perhaps you could create a feel-good folder in your inbox where you save any positive emails you've had. That might be feedback from people or team emails celebrating the successful launch of a project.

Ask our expert: Eleanor Tweddell, author of *Why Losing Your Job Could be the Best Thing That Ever Happened to You*

Coaching question: *I've been made redundant and it's really knocked my self-belief. I'm worried that I'll apply for other roles and people will think I lost my job because I'm not good enough. How can I move forward with my job search confidently?*

Expert answer: First of all, you've had a shock, it's OK to feel low. Embrace the shock and all your emotions, allow yourself time to grieve and say goodbye. It's part of moving on well. Don't put on your positive pants yet. Of course, you feel worried; don't push that away, explore it deeper. What are you worried about? What are the things that you can control and the things you can't? What are the facts, do your numbers, be very clear on what is real and what are things you just think might happen.

Your inner chatter telling you that you aren't good enough is trying to help you, it's trying to make you feel safe. But tell that chatter to dial down. You've got exciting work to do. It's time to reflect, think about what you really want to be doing. You might have some immediate needs to focus on, that's OK, focus on what you need. But don't lose sight of what you want, what your ideal tomorrow could look like and how you could start working towards it.

You can start to rebuild your confidence by looking back on your work experience so far. Remind yourself of all your achievements, the moments you loved, maybe even the moments that were tricky. Think about how you can take all the good stuff with you and leave all the harder stuff behind. Maybe this is the moment you can tell that inner chatter that you are more than good enough, you can upgrade this situation. Your next career move can be more of what you love, less of what you don't.

You now have three choices: stick, twist or bust.

1. You can stick with your expertise, and aim to upgrade in some way, such as flexible working, location, promotion.

2. You can twist, take your expertise and do it a different way, teach it, go freelance, write about it.

3. You can bust, throw everything in the air, do something completely new, retrain, start a business, chase that wild dream.

Being made redundant can rock you but it can also rock you into something even better than before. Remember what gives you energy, remember what sparks your excitement. Plenty of people are making their living doing those things. Why not you? Being made redundant could be a gift you never knew you wanted.

Not going to plan

Our careers are characterized by change and uncertainty, so it's inevitable that there will be times when things don't go to plan. When we hope something will happen and it either stalls or goes in a different direction, we all feel frustrated, if not disappointed or even angry. In these moments we can lose courage in our convictions and be unsure where to go next. We need to take actions that help us to make positive progress and move forward with momentum.

> Things don't always go to plan. You can use every hope and prayer you have, take your shot, and everything still goes to s**t. And when that happens it's almost like you never had a plan at all.
>
> **AGENT JAVIER PEÑA IN *NARCOS***

Idea for action: beginners' belief

Learning something new reminds us that we have the ability to start from scratch. Being a beginner encourages us to become comfortable with not knowing all the answers, and we often spot new ways to use our strengths too. One of the things you can always control is your curiosity, and finding opportunities to be a beginner is a great place to start. It doesn't have to be work-related learning; it can be anything that piques your interest. For example, at a time in her career when it felt like things weren't going to plan Sarah started a beginners' course in philosophy; when one of our friends was made redundant during the Covid pandemic she started a side project selling (delicious) brownies; Helen often tries out new technology to challenge herself to do things in different ways. Think about one thing you would enjoy learning from scratch.

Idea for action: write a letter to yourself

When our plans go off track it's easy to fall into rumination and regret. These negative feelings make it hard to move forward. Getting them out of our heads and onto paper can be cathartic. Write yourself a letter and pour out your frustration and disappointment (you can type your letter but writing by hand has the additional benefit of reducing stress, which is especially helpful in these moments). It doesn't have to be a letter you ever read again. You can even destroy it as soon as you have written it. Clearing your mind in this way creates the space for you to learn from the experience and look to the future.

Ask our expert: Elizabeth Uviebinené, author of *Slay in Your Lane* and *Reset*

> Confidence is a muscle. It requires lots of movement and time spent learning new things. It's not a destination.

Coaching question: *I worry so much that I'm going to get found out at work for not being able to do my job! It's making me feel really anxious. What should I do to overcome my imposter syndrome?*

Expert answer: It's important to recognize that a lot of people suffer from imposter syndrome, including people who look very successful. Whenever you feel like you're in this alone or that you're going to be found out, always remember that everyone else has felt like this as well. In fact, there are probably more people who feel like this than not.

Give yourself a break. Don't be so hard on yourself. Confidence is a muscle. It requires lots of movement and time spent learning new things. It's not a destination. It requires you to be kind to yourself. It requires you to let go of fear.

Practically, it's important to list your achievements and things you have done well in the past. It's amazing how often we forget about things we've already achieved when we look at the future with such fear that we won't be as successful again.

Self-belief requires self-acceptance. Don't try and be perfect. Understand that we're all works-in-progress and learning as we go. It's a journey. No one has it all figured out (even if it looks like they do).

Trust yourself. You are in this position for a reason.

You COACH You

You can use the COACH tool to bring together your thoughts and reflections from this chapter and apply them to the specific career challenge you might be facing at the moment. Taking the time to bring your insights together using COACH will help you to be clear about your actions, increase your confidence and spot the support you need. The more you practise using COACH, the more you'll find yourself using it for lots of different challenges both at work and in your career.

COACH

Clarity – what is your coaching challenge?

Options – what options could you explore?

Action – what actions will you take?

Confidence – how confident are you about taking those actions?

Help – what help do you need to overcome your challenge?

Summary

Self-belief: How you build the beliefs that help you succeed.

Always remember you are braver than you believe, stronger than you seem, and smarter than you think.
Christopher Robin

Why coach yourself?

Everyone experiences self-doubt, and when you understand rather than avoid or ignore those doubts you will begin to build beliefs that work for rather than against you.

Self-belief is a skill that you can learn to get better at. The stronger your self-belief the more quickly you will be able to recover from setbacks and challenge yourself to continually improve.

Coach yourself concepts

First-person vs fly-on-the-wall: Getting perspective on your challenge, particularly if you're experiencing a setback, by observing your situation from a distance.

Comfort vs courage zones: Spending time exploring your 'scary scenarios' and how increasing the amount of time in your courage zone can build your belief.

COACHING TOOLS

Building blocks of self-belief

DOING	7	8	9	
SAYING		4	5	6
THINKING	1	2	3	

Limiting to limitless lens

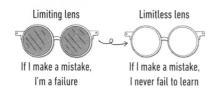

Limiting lens   Limitless lens

If I make a mistake, I'm a failure   If I make a mistake, I never fail to learn

Setback story

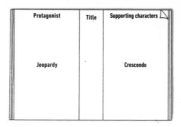

| Protagonist | Title | Supporting characters |
| Jeopardy | | Crescendo |

COACH YOURSELF QUESTIONS

1. What negative beliefs do I have that hold me back at work?
2. How have my self-doubts influenced the actions I've taken in my career?
3. What have I learnt from the setbacks that I've overcome so far?
4. How much time do I spend in my courage zone, doing things that stretch and even scare me?
5. What would I do if I knew I couldn't fail?

Listen	**Free downloads**
Squiggly Careers podcast #196 with Cate Sevilla and Rita Clifton	www.amazingif.com

I've never scored
a goal in my life
without getting
a pass from
someone else.

ABBY
WAMBACH

5 Relationships

How you create the connections you need for your career

Relationships: why coach yourself?

1. Our job satisfaction, learning and success rely on the relationships we build. Our careers don't stand still, and neither do our relationships. Quality connections are based on continual investment and focusing on what we can give as well as gain.
2. Difficult relationships have the potential to dominate our days and drain our energy. By coaching ourselves, we can better understand the role we play in conflict and repair the relationships we need in our careers.

Rewriting the role of relationships

We are collaborating in our jobs more than ever before (an increase of 50 per cent over the last decade) and the network of connections we have with our colleagues is frequently found to be the number one contributor to how engaged we are at work. David Bradford,

Ultimately, it's the quality of our relationships that will determine the quality of our lives.

ESTHER PEREL

co-author of *Connect*, says that 'work is becoming increasingly interdependent. We need others for information, resources, connections and support if we are to be successful.' Technology has made it possible to connect in an instant, and we might feel we 'know' more people than we could ever need. However, it's the quality not the quantity of our connections that impacts how much we learn, the energy we have and our ability to find our way through the tough times. Despite this, our relationships are becoming increasingly transactional. With the pressure to be 'productive' and task focused we forgo investment in relationships and even work friendships in favour of getting the job done. Margaret Heffernan points out in her book *Uncharted* that, despite strong evidence that workplace friends help senior leaders through moments of crisis in their careers, high achievers frequently let friendships fade. Heffernan says, 'It left me wondering: who will give us stamina and solidarity when the storms come?'

Repairing relationships

Despite the fact that most people come to work motivated to get along with each other, at times our differences can create difficulty. A difficult relationship can dominate our days and drain our energy. Our inclination is often to avoid addressing challenging relationships in the hope they will improve or resolve themselves. However, over time we can find ourselves becoming increasingly frustrated by friction or demotivated by disagreement.

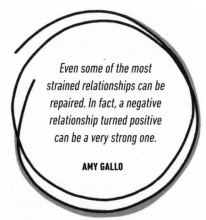

Even some of the most strained relationships can be repaired. In fact, a negative relationship turned positive can be a very strong one.

AMY GALLO

We also tend to categorize our relationships with colleagues in a black or white way, as either 'good' or 'bad'. As professors Kerry Roberts Gibson and Beth Schinoff point out in their nine years of research on workplace relationships, the reality is that most relationships are a mixed bag and they ebb and flow.[27] We make the mistake of viewing our relationships as fixed; we take the good ones for granted and believe the bad ones can never get better. Gibson and Schinoff's research on 'micromoves' found that taking small actions such as showing empathy and saying thank you has the potential to repair relationships as well as look after the ones that are going well. We have the ability to stop conflict from spiralling out of control and create the opportunity to have constructive conversations instead.

What are 'good' relationships at work?

There isn't a blueprint for building a 'good' relationship at work or the right connections for your career, but before you begin coaching yourself there are some useful principles to bear in mind; difference, distance and donate.

> *People who are open to different viewpoints will enjoy more fulfilling and successful lives.*
> **MATTHEW SYED**

Difference: cognitive diversity

Watch out for building relationships only with people who are 'a bit like you'. We might feel most comfortable spending time with people we have something in common with, but this can create an echo chamber and blind spots, where everyone thinks and sounds the same and has similar experiences. Studies have shown that teams made up of similar people tend to feel good about working together, but though they feel confident in their decisions, the decisions made are objectively worse.[28] Narrow networks limit our learning. We miss out on the different perspectives, knowledge and opportunities that other people have to offer. Building diverse relationships supports us to perform better in our jobs and improve the decisions we make about our careers.

Distance: strong and weak ties

It's helpful to make the distinction between your strong and weak ties at work. Your strong ties are the people you know well, they probably know some of the same people as you,

> *Build relationships beyond the ones that you need right now.*
>
> **MARGARET HEFFERNAN**

or work in the same area. Your strong ties are great for giving you support and a sense of belonging but are more likely to know what you already know yourself. Your weak ties are people you don't know as well and spend less time with. Mark Granovetter, a sociology professor at Stanford University, found that we often dismiss the importance of weak ties,[29] yet these are the people who bring us new knowledge, information and insights and play an important role in exploring career changes.[30] The prospect of building relationships with weak ties can feel daunting as there is a less obvious 'what's in it for them?' outcome. Reconnecting with people you've worked with or have met previously is a good way to develop your weak ties, and often easier than starting a new relationship from scratch.

Donate: generously but not selflessly

> The most meaningful way to succeed, is to help others to succeed.
>
> **ADAM GRANT**

To succeed at work we rely on other people, so it's tempting to consider our relationships by starting with what we need to gain. We need our managers to advocate for and promote us, our colleagues to make progress on our projects and our senior stakeholders to support us. However, as Adam Grant outlines in his book *Give and Take*, it is the 'givers' rather than the 'takers' who succeed in organizations. Takers exploit their relationships, are more likely to ask for and expect favours, dominate conversation and seek support without offering anything in return. Givers share their insights, expertise and connections to help others. Successful givers are not selfless, they recognize the importance of boundaries and are specific about what they can give. Givers contribute without keeping score. They are also better equipped to succeed in today's squiggly careers, as givers thrive in teams and recognize that there's room for everyone to succeed.

Thinking traps and positive prompts

Thinking traps are a useful way to identify any assumptions you have that could get in the way of being open and optimistic in your coaching approach.

〰 *We are too different from each other to have a good relationship.*
〰 *I don't have anything to offer to this relationship.*
〰 *I don't have time to build relationships outside the ones I need to do my job right now.*
〰 *That person is too senior to spend time with me.*
〰 *There is no way this person and I can work together productively; our relationship is beyond repair.*

Reframing your thinking traps as positive prompts will unlock your assumptions and give you the ability to explore options and possibilities as you coach yourself.

From: We are too different from each other to have a good relationship.
To: What could I learn from that person?

From: I don't have anything to offer to this relationship.
To: How have I built positive relationships with people in the past?

From: I don't have time to build relationships outside the ones I need to do my job right now.
To: How have I seen other people in roles like mine successfully build relationships beyond their job?

From: That person is too senior to spend time with me.
To: What do I have to offer to people who are more senior than me (strengths, experience, perspective)?

From: There is no way this person and I can work together productively; our relationship is beyond repair.
To: What do I notice about how other people work with that person?

My relationship thinking trap

_____

My relationship positive prompt

_____

How to coach yourself: relationships

In this section we will focus on how to coach yourself to create the connections you need to progress your career. We'll work through both building your connections and repairing relationships that need improving.

In Part 1 we cover:

꙳ *How to map your career community.*
꙳ *Ideas for action on how to invest in your career confidants, counsel and connections.*

In Part 2 we focus on:

꙳ *How to repair relationships with your manager through courageous conversations and empathy.*
꙳ *How to coach yourself when difference makes this difficult and the value of constructive conflict.*

The chapter ends with our expert Amy Gallo, author of *Get Along*, who shares her insights and practical advice on how to disagree with your manager in a way that can improve your relationship.

When people tell
me they've learnt
from experience, I
tell them the trick
is to learn from
other people's
experience.

WARREN
BUFFETT

PART 1: Career community: your 5 | 15 | 50

In Part 1 we will focus on how to coach yourself to review your current relationships at work, and how you can invest in the right relationships for your job today and career in the future.

The psychologist Robert Dunbar has spent his career exploring the number of relationships our brain can process at any one point in time (referred to as Dunbar's number). He suggests that on average we have around five people in our inner circle, typically family and best friends, fifteen close friends we trust, fifty friends and 150 'casual' acquaintances. Dunbar has found that his work is relevant across a wide range of settings from how armies organize themselves to the way teams work best in companies. In the next section we use Dunbar's number as inspiration for a framework to review your relationships at work, focusing on your inner circle of five career confidants, the fifteen people you trust in your career counsel and the fifty people who make up your career connections. For each group, we will support you to identify the relationships you already have, use coach yourself questions to assess the quality of those relationships and suggest ideas for action to improve your relationships. You might find some of the same people show up in your confidants, counsel and connections. This is not necessarily a bad thing, though if you have lots of overlap you could consider whether you have enough 'difference' (as we mentioned in our relationship principles) across your career community.

Your Career Community

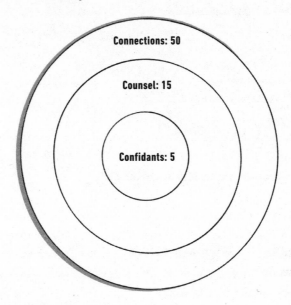

Connections: 50

Counsel: 15

Confidants: 5

Your '5': career confidants

Your career confidants are the people who probably feel more like friends than work colleagues. These relationships build organically over years, but for that to happen they still need our time and attention (as it can be easy to take these people for granted). Your career confidants are the first people you turn to in a crisis, but those shouldn't be your only moments of deep connection.

Identifying your career confidants

Use the 'who' questions below to support your reflections on who your current career confidants are:

- Who do you go to for advice if you're considering a new job opportunity?
- Who do you talk to when you're struggling with a work relationship?
- Who is the first person to celebrate your success?
- Who do you trust to tell you the truth, even if it's hard to hear?
- Who listens to you without judgement and offers you unconditional support?

My five career confidants

1. _____
2. _____
3. _____
4. _____
5. _____

Investing in your career confidants

These relationships are crucial for your career and it can be easy to assume they will always be there for you when you need them. However, like any relationship they continue to need our care and attention to stay active. Below are three ideas for action on how you can continue to build your career confidant relationships.

Idea for action: solutions, sounding board or support?

One of the best things we can do for ourselves and our confidants is to be clear about whether we need solutions, a sounding board or support. These are three distinctive needs and we respond differently to each of them. Solutions means we're searching for ideas for action, a sounding board means we'd like someone's perspective and support usually means we're looking for someone to listen to us. A great question to ask yourself before a conversation with one of your career confidants is *What do I need from this conversation, solutions, sounding board, support or something else?* You can also use this question to make sure you're giving in the most useful way to your relationships too by asking *How can I help you the most? Do you need solutions, a sounding board or support?*

Idea for action: shared problem solving

Some of your challenges could benefit from bringing a couple of your confidants together. This could be as simple as connecting a few people on a WhatsApp group or a coffee over Zoom. Asking a few of your confidants to share their perspective on your problem in a group environment can result in people building on each other's thoughts and spark new solutions. Your confidants will probably also appreciate the opportunity to make some new connections.

Idea for action: thoughtful thank yous

We find it harder to say thank you to the people we work with than in any other areas of our life.[31] We assume people know we are grateful for their support and forget the importance of saying it 'out loud'. Or sometimes it might be because saying thank you makes us feel vulnerable about needing support in the first place. When your confidants, as well as other people in your career community, have a positive impact on you, let them know. Thanking people for their help also increases the likelihood of that person helping others as they're reminded of the positive impact they can have.

> *Appreciation can change a day, even change a life. Your willingness to put it into words is all that is necessary.*
>
> **MARGARET COUSINS**

One action I'm going to take in the next month to invest in my career confidants:

_____

Your '15': career counsel

The fifteen (or so) people in your career counsel offer you support, spot opportunities on your behalf and give you constructive challenge. This group might include mentors, managers (past and present), peers and people from the networks that you belong to.

The next exercise is designed to help you review your current counsel and whether you have the right mix of people in place. Start by listing the people who are in your career counsel in the table on the next page (don't worry if you don't have fifteen yet). Now ask yourself these four questions to come up with their profile:

1. Does the person support you more in doing your current job or in exploring future career opportunities?
2. Is this person more of a challenger who asks you hard questions or a supporter who builds your belief?

3. Is this person from outside your world (i.e. your industry / company) or someone who can empathize with your experiences?
4. Is this person similar to you (do you have shared points of view / values) or do you often have different ideas or even disagree?

Though some people in your counsel will be able to do both of the things listed in the profile, e.g. both support you with your current job and explore future opportunities, the idea with this exercise is to work out their more prominent role.

Your Career Counsel					
Name	Current/ Future? (C/F)	Challenger/ Supporter? (C/S)	Outsider/ Empathizer? (O/E)	Different/ Similar? (D/S)	Profile
Example *Rob as one of Sarah's '15'*	C	C	E	S	CCES
1					
2					
3					
4					
5					
6					
7					
8					
9					
10					
11					
12					
13					
14					
15					

Now you have profiled your career counsel, look at the final column in the table. What do you notice? The best career counsels have a diverse mix of support, so any areas where you have too much 'sameness' represent an opportunity to take action. For example, as we discussed at the start of this chapter it's not uncommon to realize you have a career counsel full of people who are similar to you. Or, if you're someone who, like Sarah, finds conflict difficult, you might be missing people who challenge you in your counsel. Before moving on to the idea for action ask yourself three coach yourself questions:

CY? What has helped me to build relationships with the people on my counsel?

_____

CY? What roles are missing from my career counsel?

_____

CY? Who could help me to fill the roles I need most on my counsel (either directly or through introductions)?

_____

Idea for action: spot the difference

It can be hard to find and build relationships with people who are different from you. One way to get better at this is to spend time with people who have differing points of view, both from you and from each other. It might be someone who makes decisions that you disagree with or who offers a perspective you hadn't considered before. These people sometimes seem slightly scary from a distance as their approach feels unfamiliar, but they can become some of your most valuable career counsel members. They are the people most likely to stop you in your tracks or say something that surprises you. You don't need to agree with

> It's a very important thing to learn to talk to people you disagree with.
>
> **PETE SEEGER**

someone to have a positive relationship with them. To build a relationship with a person who is different from you, it can be useful to start with what we call a 'challenge-and-build' approach. The challenge-and-build approach involves three stages:

1. Identify the project or task where you would appreciate some additional perspectives or constructive criticism.
2. Approach the people you would like to spend time with, sharing a summary of your project and let them know you would appreciate their challenge-and-build when you next have time together.
3. Keep challenge-and-build meetings small, ideally one to one and only up to a maximum of four (including you). Any more than this and it can be hard to keep track and control of conversations.

We have both used this approach in our careers and found it useful. Not only do you build relationships with a wider range of people but these types of meetings also do a great job of helping you to build your influence within an organization.

One action I'm going to take in the next month to invest in my career counsel:

_____

Your '50': career connections

Your career connections are not just fifty people you happen to know; instead they are fifty people who are playing an important role in your career right now. You might see them less frequently than your confidants or counsel, but you know who they are and how and when you would go to them for input, support or advice. The next exercise will help you to see all your connections in one place and will be useful to refer back to as you consider which relationships you want to invest in, and where there are new relationships you need to build.

How to identify your career connections

—ℓ→ Start mapping your connections by answering each of the 'who' questions we've suggested on the next page.

—ℓ→ Write the names of the people rather than general phrases, for example rather than writing 'previous manager' you would write their name.

—ℓ→ Some people will probably appear more than once, for example your manager might also be your mentor. A colleague could both be helping you do your job and be a friend.

—ℓ→ Remember to include people in and out of your current organization in your career community.

—ℓ→ You might have some people in your career community who don't 'fit' under any of the 'who' questions, and you can add these people to the 'who else' question.

My career connections

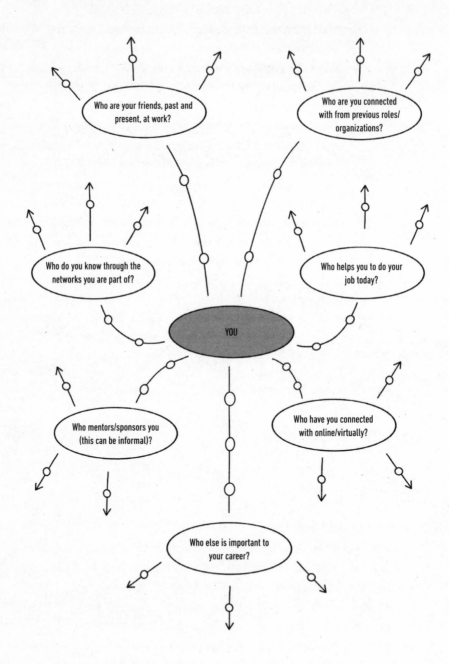

Number of people in my career connections ———

Reflecting on your career connections, note down your thoughts on each of the following coach yourself questions.

CY? What do I notice after mapping my career connections?

——————————————————————————————

CY? Who would I like to build a stronger relationship with?

——————————————————————————————

CY? Where are the biggest gaps in my career connections?

——————————————————————————————

Keeping your career connections engaged and active

Maintaining multiple relationships is hard work, so it's important to find small ways you can stay regularly connected with people. We've shared two ideas for action on how you can invest in your career connections in a sustainable way.

Idea for action: the five-minute favour

Five-minute favours are simple and quick ways to support people, without expecting anything in return. If you did a five-minute favour every day for two months, by the end you could have given something small to all fifty people in your career community. This is a great giving habit to practise, and the more you do it the easier it becomes to spot opportunities to offer support. Some examples of five-minute favours that we both do frequently include:

No act of kindness, however small, is wasted.

AESOP

1. Sending someone an article/podcast/book you think they'll be interested in.
2. Connecting two people in your career community.
3. Writing a LinkedIn recommendation.
4. Giving strengths-based feedback, *I thought you were brilliant in that meeting because* . . .
5. Sending a video message or voice note to someone to give them support or encouragement.

Idea for action: support at scale

Giving something of value to as many of your connections as possible at the same time is a smart use of your time and your strengths. For example, Helen writes a newsletter called *Squiggly Careers Curiosity*, which she publishes on LinkedIn as a way of sharing with her connections the knowledge and ideas she has on different topics. In a similar way one of our friends, James Whatley, writes a brilliant newsletter called *Five Things on a Friday*. For the benefit of his connections, James curates articles, videos and opinions on relevant and timely topics. Support at scale doesn't only work with your external connections. One of the people in our workshops ran 'Coding 101' lunchtime learning sessions that were open to anyone in his organization who wanted to learn more about basic coding skills.

> **One action I'm going to take in the next month to invest in my career counsel:**
>
> _____

Career acquaintances – what about the 150?

You might have noticed we haven't included the 150 'casual acquaintances' in our community tool. In the context of your career this group is harder to map and manage but you can influence the flow of casual career acquaintances that could become connections in the future. A good place to start is to spend some time every couple of months in new places and spaces and make time for curious conversations. For Helen, this might happen by connecting with people on LinkedIn or through Lunchclub.com. For Sarah, it could look like being introduced to new networks by people already in her career community.

CY? Where do I currently spend time that could help me meet casual career acquaintances that could become part of my future career community?

_____

CY? How could I explore new places and spaces to have curious conversations that might spark new relationships in my career community in the future?

_____

PART 2: Repairing relationships

Despite our best efforts, there are times when work relationships go wrong. Disagreements can create friction; different ways of working can lead to disconnection and a lack of empathy and respect can even mean we start to dislike the people we work with. None of this makes us feel good about our work. In Part 2 of this chapter we focus on two of the most common relationship challenges at work: a bad or broken relationship with a manager and uncomfortable friction with a colleague. All the tools and ideas for action we share can also be used to coach yourself through any relationship challenge you're experiencing at work.

Managers matter

Our managers have a disproportionate impact on how we feel about work, and studies suggest that around 70 per cent of our engagement depends directly on who we work for.[32] A broken, disconnected or distant manager relationship can dominate our days and distract us from doing good work. It can even mean we change jobs. Market research company Gallup found that 50 per cent of us leave a job because of a manager at some point in our careers.[33]

Courageous conversations

One of the first ways in which you can rebuild a relationship with your manager is by having a courageous conversation. This will feel challenging for most people as it takes bravery to bring up a difficult topic when you don't know what the response will be. Courageous conversations require curiosity, clarity and confidence. The idea for action below can help you prepare for these conversations.

Idea for action: sort the situation

Sharing feedback with your manager about the impact of their approach, actions or behaviours can feel difficult, but it is undoubtedly one of the most effective ways of moving friction forward. Our SORT framework is a helpful way to prepare for a courageous conversation and gives you a sense of direction in the discussion. SORT stands for:

Situation – what is happening at the moment?
Observation – what actions/behaviours do you see?
Reaction – how is this making you feel?
Together – how can we move things forward together?

You don't have to follow this rigidly when you're talking to your manager. It's important that the discussion feels more like a conversation than a confrontation, but knowing what you want to say and practising beforehand can help you to feel more confident in the moment.

Practising empathy with your manager

When our relationship with our manager isn't working well it can feel like we're in a fight, and an 'us versus them' mindset can take over. While this is understandable, it's not helpful. Instead of seeing your manager as the enemy, it's more constructive to take the opportunity to practise empathy. The School of Life describes empathy as 'not opposed to our own interests but an essential resource for doing what we want more successfully'. Neuroscience also suggests that empathy is effective as mirror neurons in our brains naturally prompt people to reciprocate behaviours. So, if you can start empathizing with your manager, you increase the chance that they will do the same for you. As philosopher Roman Krznaric points out in his book *Empathy*, there is only so much progress you can make by thinking about empathy: 'We can learn it best when we leave the manuals behind and set out on experiential adventures.'

We've suggested two ideas for action that you can start putting into practice straight away: switching positions and understudy skills.

Idea for action: switching positions

Switching positions allows you to see things from your manager's perspective. This insight can help you to pre-empt the challenges your manager might have and allows you to be more proactive in your suggestions and solutions. Answer the coach yourself questions below to begin thinking about your manager's mindset at the moment.

CY? What might be keeping my manager awake at night?

_____

CY? How does my manager spend the majority of their time?

_____

CY? What motivates and drives my manager?

_____

CY? If I was in my manager's position what would I think, feel and do in this situation?

_____

Idea for action: understudy skills

Managers are often juggling different priorities and pressures on top of managing the people in their team. They need to deliver projects and initiatives as well as making the time to direct and develop the people who work for them. It's not an easy job to do well and without understanding the other elements of their job it can be hard to empathize fully with them. One very practical way you can learn more about your manager's role is to try doing a part of it. This could be by deputizing for your manager in some meetings when they're away on holiday, or offering to help on a project if your manager has too much on at the moment. This is not as intimidating as it initially sounds as people don't usually expect you to 'be' your manager, but you get a good insight into the reality of their role.

One way I'm going to start practising empathy with my manager:

_____

The reality of repairing a bad manager relationship

If you start having courageous conversations and practising empathy in an effort to repair and restore your relationship with your manager, you will hopefully soon see the green shoots of progress. Those green shoots might show up as enjoying more of your conversations together, learning from your manager or being able to anticipate where your manager needs help. Occasionally you might do all the right things and the relationship doesn't improve. In this instance it's good to set yourself a time limit on how long you're prepared to continue investing in the relationship before you start seeking other options. Even if you're planning to move on you can still use that time productively to build relationships and learn as much as you can.

Dealing with difficult people

At times in our careers, we all work with people we find difficult and perhaps even dread spending time with. There are two common reasons why we find people difficult:

1. They think and behave differently from us.
2. They actively and openly disagree with us.

We've explored each of these below and shared ideas for action to help you to coach yourself to improve these relationships.

When difference makes things difficult

We all bring our own insights, assumptions and approaches to work. It's what makes us unique and different. Difference is valuable because it leads to creative outcomes and helps to solve problems. It also causes friction when people think and behave in a way that jars with how we see the world. Friction can show up in small and frustrating ways, like being interrupted when you're talking, or be significant and stall your progress, such as someone excluding you from meetings.

Our personality impacts our interactions. Complementary personalities find it easy to bond and this often creates a sense of belonging. Conflicting personalities, on the other hand, can lead to difficulty and distress. There are lots of psychometric profiling tools that help us to 'categorize' ourselves and the people we work with (such as DISC or Insights Discovery). Each of these tools can help you to understand where personalities might be complementary or create conflict. We've used some of the principles behind them to create a simple way for you to diagnose your difficult relationships and help you to think about your most effective response.

What shape do you show up as?

Look at the four shapes and their descriptions in the table on the next page. As a warning, none of these descriptions are particularly appealing but the purpose of this exercise is to identify how you and other people behave under the pressure of a difficult relationship, and that is very rarely us at our best. No one shape is better than another at dealing with difficult relationships.

The heated hexagon

Behaviours you might spot
Getting fixed on a perspective. Acting first and listening later. Prioritizes progress over people. Can be snappy, impatient and demanding of others.

Words you might say
We're overthinking this.
We need to move on.

The data based diamond

Behaviours you might spot
Interrogating information and deep-diving into details. Prioritizes evidence over empathy. Can be stubborn and stall progress.

Words you might say
We need more data and detail.
Where's your proof?

The talkative triangle

Behaviours you might spot
Talks too much and too fast. Gets excited and emotional. Prioritizes feelings over facts. Opinionated and argumentative if feeling excluded.

Words you might say
You don't understand.
This is a disaster.

The consensus seeking circle

Behaviours you might spot
Uncomfortable making decisions. Dislikes being put on the spot. Prioritizes consensus over questions. Cautious and can withdraw into themselves under pressure.

Words you might say
What do you think?
As long as you're happy, I'm happy.

Now you've familiarized yourself with the shapes and their profiles, answer the questions below:

CY? What shape do I show up as in a difficult relationship?

_____

CY? What behaviours do I recognize in myself when dealing with a difficult relationship?

_____

CY? What sort of phrases might I say?

_____

CY? What shape of person do I typically find most difficult?

_____

CY? If I am experiencing a difficult relationship right now, what shape do I think the other person is?

_____

Fixing friction

Now that you have understood your response to difficult relationships and thought more about the people you work with, you can start identifying what actions you might take to improve a relationship. This doesn't mean you have to pretend to be someone else or 'change shape'; the focus is on small adaptations you can make to your approach that could have a big impact on your relationship. The table on the next page helps you to start this process by plotting your shape against someone else's. You can then spot what your relationship risks are and how you could respond to those risks.

		What shape are they?			
		Heated hexagon	Data based diamond	Talkative triangle	Consensus seeking circle
What shape are you?	**Heated hexagon**	**Risk** You both think you're right and conversation gets heated. **Response** Switch your approach to understanding and listening.	**Risk** You want to move on and they want to dive into the detail. **Response** Be clear about deadlines. Ask them to share recommendations.	**Risk** They feel frustrated by your lack of positive energy. **Response** Make time for informal chats within meetings.	**Risk** They become irritated because you're not including people. **Response** Proactively ask for people's ideas and inputs before moving on.
	Data based diamond	**Risk** You want to get to the right answer, but they want to get it done and move on. **Response** Understand what is important to them and how your insight and data could be helpful.	**Risk** You get stuck in analysis paralysis and duplicate each other's work. **Response** Agree clear deadlines, expectations, roles and responsibilities.	**Risk** You get frustrated by a lack of focus and they think you're being negative. **Response** Help them understand how your approach can make things bigger and better.	**Risk** They think your facts don't reflect people's feelings and challenge your approach. **Response** Combine their insights and your data to create a more compelling outcome.

What shape are they?			
Heated hexagon	Data based diamond	Talkative triangle	Consensus seeking circle

What shape are you?

Talkative triangle

	Heated hexagon	Data based diamond	Talkative triangle	Consensus seeking circle
Risk	You frustrate them with a lack of focus.	You get bored and distracted and they see it as disrespectful.	You talk about a lot but don't get anything done.	You lose energy when they want to spend time to gain consensus.
Response	Ask them to be clear about what needs to happen by when and how you can help.	Have short meetings which focus on priority problems and metrics which matter most.	Agree to divide your meeting equally between catching up and moving things forward.	Generate ideas for things that could be done quickly and which would support their agenda.

Consensus seeking circle

	Heated hexagon	Data based diamond	Talkative triangle	Consensus seeking circle
Risk	They dismiss your input and you judge them for being impatient and insensitive.	They come across as confrontational and argumentative, which makes you withdraw.	You find them overdramatic and tune out when they speak.	You both see things could improve but a mutual avoidance of conflict means nothing changes.
Response	Follow-up meetings with reflections and suggestions you may not have been able to share in the moment.	Ask them open questions to shift their attention from facts/data to insight e.g. 'What does "good" look like?'	Actively listen with the intention of sharing key messages so everyone is on the same page.	Focus on small actions and outcomes: 'What's one small thing we could both do that would make a difference?'

CY? What action could I take to reduce the friction in my relationships?

When disagreement makes things difficult

Disagreement doesn't always have to be difficult, and conflict doesn't have to feel like combat. Conflict expert Amy Gallo has found that constructive conflict leads to better work outcomes, opportunities to learn and grow, a higher level of job satisfaction and a more inclusive work environment.[34] Coaching ourselves on our response to conflict is an important part of building effective relationships at work.

Are you an activator or avoider?

Before we can work out how to spend more time in the useful 'middle ground' of constructive conflict, it's important to know whether you're naturally more of a conflict activator or avoider. You might have a sense straight away but there's a more detailed description below to help you reflect further.

ACTIVATOR	AVOIDER
Most likely to say *'Lets talk about this now.'* *'I disagree.'*	**Most likely to say** *'Shall we pick this up later?'* *'It's not a problem.'*
Most likely to do Send emails in the heat of the moment. Stand up when they are talking. Dominate conversations.	**Most likely to do** Get defensive and withdraw. Complain outside the meeting. Disguise their feelings with humour.

Answer the questions on the next page on your own style of conflict and consider how this relates to the people you work for and with.

Where do you sit on the conflict scale?

ACTIVATOR   AVOIDER

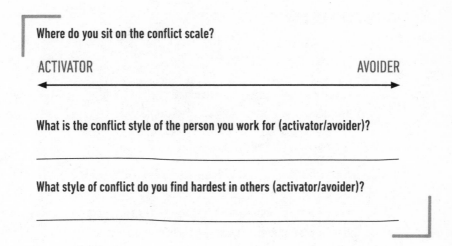

What is the conflict style of the person you work for (activator/avoider)?

_____

What style of conflict do you find hardest in others (activator/avoider)?

_____

Below are some ideas for action for creating the middle ground of constructive conflict where everyone can contribute.

Activator + activator

These conversations are likely to be full of conflict, debate and discussion but not much resolution. Each person will stick to their argument and will find it hard to compromise. Activators also dominate conversations so you miss out on other people's perspectives.

Idea for action: start with structure

Activators benefit from rules of engagement. Creating a clear structure helps everyone to be heard and keeps people on track. This can be as specific as starting a meeting by giving everyone five minutes to share their point of view on a topic, followed by fifteen minutes of discussion, and then agreeing on priorities and actions. If a neutral person is allocated to facilitate conversations that can also be helpful to make sure a conversation progresses with the right pace and purpose.

Activator + avoider

This conversation will be frustrating for everyone involved. Activators are looking for a good debate and at the same time avoiders are trying their utmost to make sure that doesn't happen! This can result in activators going full steam ahead on a task, without agreement from avoiders, who at their worst can even silently undermine progress from behind the scenes.

Idea for action: start with support

This is where everyone needs to meet in the middle. Activators need to lean out to give avoiders space and avoiders need to lean in to engage with the conversation. For activators this might mean focusing on listening and avoiding interrupting other people. For avoiders it might mean asking questions and offering options to consider. One way to find common ground is to understand what outcomes are important to both people and explore ways you can work together to support each other rather than conflict becoming combative.

Avoider + avoider

These conversations will stall as no one is prepared to share their point of view. You also might not even recognize that you're disagreeing with each other, which is an additional challenge to be aware of.

Idea for action: start with scenarios

To encourage everyone to participate in the conversation you can use scenarios to prompt discussion. For example, you could use a meeting to explore three different directions a project could take and ask everyone to share their pros and cons for each different route. This feels like a 'safe' way for people who usually avoid conflict to engage in and even enjoy conversations where people are sharing their respective points of view. Getting avoiders to share their thoughts over email before a discussion can also help to move a conversation forward.

Look for the middle-ground mediators

There are some people who aren't avoiders or activators of conflict; instead constructive conflict is one of their strengths. You can learn a lot from watching these 'middle-ground mediators' in action. They are calm and assertive with the skill to navigate conversations even if they take an unexpected turn. Mediators will spot if someone is being left out of the conversation and effectively defuse tension when it arises. Think about who are the middle-ground meditators you work with today and what they do well. You could even approach them directly to ask for hints and tips to improve your approach to constructive conflict.

Ask our expert: Amy Gallo, author of *Get Along: Eight Types of Difficult People and How to Work with Them*

While disagreeing with someone more powerful than you can be nerve-racking, when you do it with respect and confidence, it can improve your work and your relationship.

Coaching question: *How can I disagree with my manager without coming across as difficult or disrespectful?*

Expert answer: Your manager's opinion of you matters a lot. After all, they have power over important aspects of your work life – where and when you work, what projects you get to take on, your salary, and your future at the organization.

Of course, it's just plain easier to agree with your manager – and, let's be honest, that's what some bosses want – but not speaking up can have harmful consequences and lead to missed opportunities. Here's what you can do instead of being a yes-person.

Flip the risk assessment
Our natural inclination is to think of all the things that could go terribly wrong if we voice our opinion. But don't start there. Instead, consider the risks of *not* speaking up first. Perhaps the project will be derailed or you'll lose the team's trust. Then weigh those against the potential consequences of saying something. Be realistic. Some concern is valid, but chances are you're not going to get fired or make a lifelong enemy.

Ask permission to disagree
Broach the topic by assessing whether your manager is open to hearing what you have to say. Explain that you have a different opinion and ask if you can voice it: 'I see this differently. Would it be OK for me to lay out my thoughts?' This may seem overly deferential, but it gives your boss a sense of control, rather than catching them off guard. It's rare that a leader will say no to this type of question, but if they do, then you know where you stand. And, assuming they say yes, now that they've verbally opted in, you'll feel more confident sharing your disagreement.

Steer away from judgements
Restate your manager's point of view so it's clear you understand it. Speak confidently and slowly – talking in an even tone calms you and the other person down. Then share your opinion, stating the facts and avoiding any judgement words, such as 'hasty', 'foolish' or 'wrong', that might annoy your manager. Simply express your point of view and be open to having a conversation about it.

Respect their authority
Ultimately, your manager is probably going to make the final decision, so acknowledge that. You might say, 'I know you'll make the call here and I wanted to add my thoughts.' At the same time, don't be obsequious and undermine yourself. Good managers want people to have opinions, even ones that don't jibe with theirs.

The good news is that when you've done this once, it'll be easier to do the next time. While disagreeing with someone more powerful than you can be nerve-racking, when you do it with respect and confidence, it can improve your work and your relationship.

You COACH You

You can use the COACH tool to bring together your thoughts and reflections from this chapter and apply them to the specific career challenge you might be facing at the moment. Taking the time to bring your insights together using COACH will help you to be clear about your actions, increase your confidence and spot the support you need. The more you practise using COACH, the more you'll find yourself using it for lots of different challenges both at work and in your career.

COACH

Clarity – what is your coaching challenge?

Options – what options could you explore?

Action – what actions will you take?

Confidence – how confident are you about taking those actions?

Help – what help do you need to overcome your challenge?

Summary

Relationships: How to create the connections you need for your career.

I've never scored a goal in my life without getting a pass from someone else.
Abby Wambach

Why coach yourself?

Your job satisfaction, learning and success rely on the quality of the relationships you build.

Difficult relationships have the potential to dominate your days and drain your energy. By understanding yourself and other people you can repair relationships and benefit from constructive challenge.

Coach yourself concepts

Building your career community based on three principles:

Difference: Creating diverse connections that offer you new ideas and perspectives.

Distance: Investing in people who support and empathize with you (strong ties) and people who know things you don't (weak ties).

Donate: Developing strong relationships by starting with what you have to give.

COACHING TOOLS

Career community

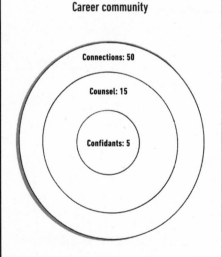

Connections: 50

Counsel: 15

Confidants: 5

Understanding difference

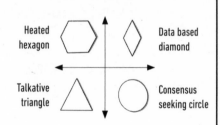

Heated hexagon

Data based diamond

Talkative triangle

Consensus seeking circle

Fixing friction

Middle-ground mediator

COACH YOURSELF QUESTIONS

1. What has helped me to build relationships in my career so far?
2. What do I have to give to the connections I'd like to create?
3. How much effort do I spend maintaining existing relationships vs building new ones?
4. What relationships do I find difficult?
5. How could I learn from people who have different skills, perspectives and experiences from me?

Listen	Free downloads
Squiggly Careers podcast #146 with Amy Gallo	www.amazingif.com

Deep human
connection is . . . the
purpose and the result
of a meaningful life.

MELINDA
GATES

We keep moving
forward, opening up
new doors and doing
new things, because
we're curious . . . and
curiosity keeps leading
us down new paths.

WALT
DISNEY

6 ⟿ Progression

Moving forward with momentum

Progression: why coach yourself

1. Being proactive about our progression gives us options and makes our careers more change-proof.
2. Taking ownership of our progression increases the control we have over our careers and makes our development less dependent on other people.

Proactive progression

> The reason I don't have a plan is because if I have a plan, I'm limited to today's options.
>
> **SHERYL SANDBERG**

Career progression is about much more than promotion; it's how we continually move forward in our careers. If we stand still we become vulnerable to the changes that are happening around us. The lifespan of a skill is now estimated to be five years or less. This means that even if you stay in the same role for the next five years your current knowledge is unlikely to be enough to enable you to do your job brilliantly.[35] When we make progress in our careers, we increase our options, adaptability and opportunities. We build our confidence by unlearning and relearning, building and starting from scratch, experimenting and exploring. Progression helps us to be more change-proof and comfortable with the curve balls that come our way.

Owning your career

One of the challenges of working in an environment that is always on, and where our to-do lists are rarely done, is that our day jobs can get in the way of our longer-term development. We hope, or expect, that a progression opportunity will be presented to us as an inevitable result of the hard work and efforts we're investing day to day. The challenge with this approach is that we are delegating our career development to other people and relying on forces and factors outside our control. We can then start to feel frustrated, resentful and stuck when we don't see the progression we are looking for. Taking ownership of your career gives you control over how you grow and where you go. You don't have to wait for other people to come to you with a new role or project to get involved in; instead you create your own opportunities.

What is progression?

Progression used to mean climbing the ladder. We worked to a one-size-fits-all view of success and our job was to follow in the footsteps of the people who went before us. Learning was limited to what you needed to know to get to the next level. Progression was predictable and our possibilities were few and far between. With companies continually pivoting and adapting, the linear path has been replaced with something much more fluid, as our careers now flow in lots of different directions. Career progression is personal and unique to you. There is no blueprint to follow, and progression means many different things, from learning new skills to redesigning how you work to developing as a manager. Being proactive about your progression will give you more opportunities to grow, explore and discover new directions in your career.

Every success story
is a tale of constant
adaption, revision
and change.

**RICHARD
BRANSON**

Progression pressure vs progressing at your own pace

When reflecting on your progress you might start to feel what we call 'progression pressure', a sense that you're not doing enough. That might be sparked by following people on social media who seem to be succeeding in their job, starting a side project and learning a new skill all at the same time. Or perhaps you feel that your peers or friends, at least on the surface, seem like you 'only better'. However, no two careers are the same, and don't forget we all have a tendency to share our 'highlights reel' when describing our progress to other people.[36] Your pace of progression is personal to you and will vary at different points in your career. As you coach yourself through this chapter you shouldn't feel any pressure to progress for progression's sake but find yourself feeling excited about how you can move forward in your own way.

Ready-made rewards vs personalized progression

The traditional career ladder came with lots of 'ready-made rewards': grades, bonuses, promotions and impressive job titles could be collected and added to your work wall of fame (aka your CV). Over time, we've all become reliant on these ready-made rewards as signals of our progress. However, these rewards are misleading as they rarely lead to better performance.[37] Instead of helping us to continually grow and develop, they dramatically reduce our creativity and, as the late Cornell University professor John Condry put it, they are the 'enemies of exploration'. Our relationship with ready-made rewards has been reinforced over time by teachers, parents and managers. We have got used to an 'if you do this, then you get that' way of thinking. The pursuit of these rewards is not progression. They might *result* from our progression, but they are only one part of how we progress.

Thinking traps and positive prompts

Thinking traps are a useful way to identify any assumptions you have that could get in the way of being open and optimistic in your coaching approach.

I need to be promoted in order to progress.

If I stay still, I'm going to stop learning.

At this stage in my career, I should have made more progress (be more senior/ be paid more money/have more responsibility).

It's not possible to progress without sacrificing other aspects of my life (flexibility, family etc.).

I want to do something different, but it will mean going backwards.

Going from thinking traps to positive prompts will unlock your assumptions and give you the ability to explore options and possibilities as you coach yourself.

From: I need to be promoted in order to progress.
To: What are three ways, other than being promoted, that I could progress at work?

From: If I stay still, I'm going to stop learning.
To: How might I create new opportunities to grow in my current role?

From: At this stage in my career, I should have made more progress.
To: What am I proud of achieving in my career so far?

From: It's not possible to progress without sacrificing other aspects of my life.
To: What could I invest time in now, so my progression is there for me when I feel ready for it?

From: I want to do something different, but it will mean going backwards.
To: How could a move backwards now, help me to move forward in the future?

My progression thinking trap

My progression positive prompt

How to coach yourself on progression

If you're coaching yourself on progression you will probably be starting with one or both of these thoughts: *I'm interested in exploring my progression possibilities* and/or *I have an idea what progression looks like for me and need some help to make it happen*. We have structured this section in two parts so you can work through both of these areas.

In Part 1 we will explore:

↪ *What progression means to you.*
↪ *How to identify lots of different options and opportunities to progress.*
↪ *How to prioritize the progression that matters most to you right now.*

In Part 2 we'll move on to how you can take action on your progression priorities including:

↪ *How to prototype your progression.*
↪ *How to secure the support you need to progress.*

We finish the chapter with our expert Adam Morgan, author of *A Beautiful Constraint*, who shares how a stubbornly adaptive mindset and the can-if method can support you when your progression stalls.

PART 1: Finding your meaning in momentum

When we understand our own motivations for progression it stops being something that we feel we 'should' or 'have to' do and starts being something we're excited about and that gives us energy. To start figuring out what feels meaningful for you, use the space on the next page to note down three examples of how you've made progress in your career so far. Then, next to each example write down the upsides and downsides of each experience. To support your reflections we've included a few of Sarah's progression examples below.

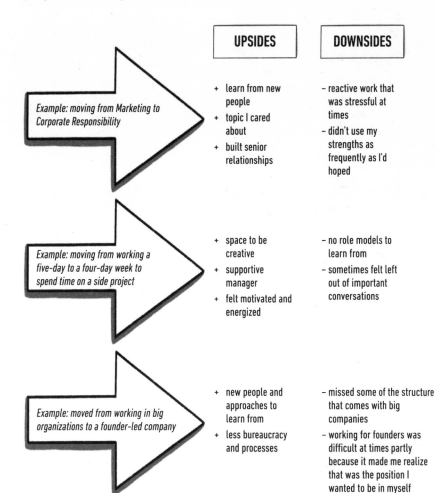

UPSIDES

DOWNSIDES

Example: moving from Marketing to Corporate Responsibility

+ learn from new people
+ topic I cared about
+ built senior relationships

– reactive work that was stressful at times
– didn't use my strengths as frequently as I'd hoped

Example: moving from working a five-day to a four-day week to spend time on a side project

+ space to be creative
+ supportive manager
+ felt motivated and energized

– no role models to learn from
– sometimes felt left out of important conversations

Example: moved from working in big organizations to a founder-led company

+ new people and approaches to learn from
+ less bureaucracy and processes

– missed some of the structure that comes with big companies
– working for founders was difficult at times partly because it made me realize that was the position I wanted to be in myself

EXAMPLE OF MY PROGRESSION	UPSIDES	DOWNSIDES

1.

+ _____
+ _____
+ _____

- _____
- _____
- _____

2.

+ _____
+ _____
+ _____

- _____
- _____
- _____

3.

+ _____
+ _____
+ _____

- _____
- _____
- _____

We now want to use your progression examples (don't feel limited to three – the more the better) to consider why progression matters to you. To help you answer this question use the table below to circle any words that connect with you when you think about this. As you reflect, you might come up with new words that feel right for you, so we've left space for you to add these in.

Why progression matters to me			
Success	Pride	Meaning	Achievement
Impact	Productivity	Recognition	Ambition
Fulfilment	Potential	Direction	Worth
Purpose	Momentum	Improving	Accomplishment
Significance	Status	Joy	Influence
Control	Importance	Learning	Opportunity
Growth			

Use your notes from the above exercises to consider each of the following coach yourself (CY) questions:

CY? Which examples of progression feel the most meaningful to me?

_____

_____

CY? Why do those examples stand out as the most positive?

_____

_____

CY? Which examples of progression feel the least meaningful to me?

_____

_____

CY? Why do those examples stand out as not feeling as positive as the others?

_____

_____

CY? What words connected with me when I asked myself why progression matters to me?

_____

_____

Before we move on to exploring your progression possibilities, summarize your reflections so far using the following statement:

Progression matters to me because

_____

_____

Your progression possibilities

As you coach yourself through the next exercise explore as many options, ambitions and ideas as you can come up with. There are no limits, filters or practicalities at this point (they come later). You shouldn't ignore obvious options but the intention with this exercise is to go beyond what is straight ahead of you. When you think you've run out of ideas, go for a walk, take a shower, make a coffee and see if a change of scenery sparks a new thought.

Your planets of progression

This exercise is to help you visualize all the potential progression possibilities in your career solar system. Some possibilities might feel very familiar whereas others are ventures into the unknown. At this stage there are no constraints on where your career could take you.

Step 1: Write down as many progression possibilities around 'Planet You' as you can think of.

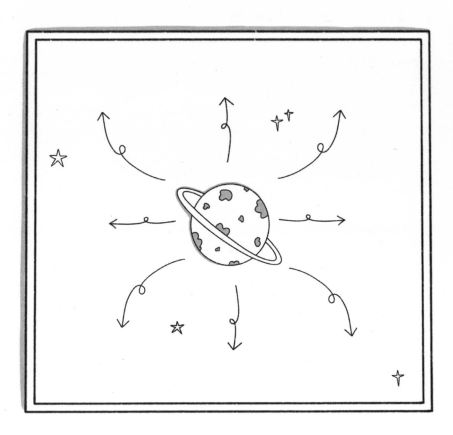

Step 2: Now that you've started exploring your progression possibilities have a look at the examples below and see if there are any that you'd like to add to your solar system.

Progression possibilities – examples		
Secondment	Job crafting	Work redesign
Learning opportunities	Promotion	Side project
Job swap	Management	Mentoring
Internal projects	Shadowing	Volunteering
Personal brand building	Creating a new role	Sideways move

Progression possibilities – our examples

Below we've shared some examples of how progression possibilities have worked in practice for both of us. These progression possibilities weren't presented to us, we made them happen because they were important to us and our careers. The risk with these kinds of short 'success' stories is they make it sound easy, but each of these examples took commitment, time and some creative thinking along the way.

Creating a new role

We both spent two years on a university placement programme at the UK health and beauty retailer Boots. Everyone on the programme did a series of six-month rotations that were predetermined by HR.

Sarah saw an opportunity to take a different approach and contacted a supplier that worked with Boots to create a new rotation role to broaden her commercial experience. Sarah's approach was innovative and created progression possibilities that didn't exist previously.

Sideways move

Helen joined an energy company called E.ON and within three months of starting at the company made a horizontal move into a new function that better aligned with her skills and expertise. She did this by building a relationship with the manager of the function she was interested in and discussing how her abilities could support the team's work. Transitioning to a new role so quickly after joining a company was counter to the standard progression path. Helen made it happen by creating a clear transition plan and securing the support she needed from stakeholders internally.

Work redesign

During her time at British supermarket chain Sainsbury's, Sarah renegotiated her working pattern to enable her to continue in her leadership role and take a day a week to work on the development of our business, Amazing If. This was a pioneering approach to career management within Sainsbury's, where this sort of role flexibility had previously been used predominantly by parents. Sarah created a plan of how her role could be achieved in a four-day week and benefited from the belief and trust she had built with her team, in particular her manager.

Learning opportunities

During her time at Capital One and Virgin, Helen pitched for investment in her learning when she realized that other forms of progression weren't available to her at the time. She researched courses that would support her career development, created a business case to outline the companies' return on investment (this included her training other people in the business by passing on what she had learnt) and pitched it to senior managers. After lots of conversations, Helen unlocked previously unavailable funding, enabling her to study subjects and secure qualifications that have furthered her career over the long term.

Volunteering

Sarah wanted to spend more time supporting people's career development, so she set up a volunteer group called Inspire. The Inspire team put on leadership events that raised money to support young people at the start of their careers who came from disadvantaged backgrounds. This is one of Sarah's most positive progression examples. It gave her the opportunity to learn from different people, develop her strengths in new ways and increase her impact.

Prioritizing your progression

You probably have lots of different progression possibilities that feel appealing. While you can progress in more than one direction at once, it's also good to be realistic about how much you can achieve at any one moment. To help you prioritize your progression possibilities there are two questions to consider:

1. How energized and excited are you about the possibility?
2. How well does your possibility fit with what's important to you about progression (it might be useful to refer back to your 'Why progression matters to me' answer)?

To compare and contrast each of your progression possibilities, plot them on the matrix opposite based on your answers to the two questions above. You might have lots of possibilities in one section of the matrix and none in others. There is no 'right' answer.

Prioritizing your progression

ENERGY (HIGH)

SHINY
OBJECTS

PRIORITIES

FIT (LOW)

FIT (HIGH)

STOP

HARD TO DO

ENERGY (LOW)

Where your possibilities lie on the energy / fit matrix informs how you approach exploring them. On the next page we share the actions we'd recommend for each area of the matrix: Priorities; Shiny Objects; Stop; and Hard to Do's.

Priorities = start prototyping and securing support

These are the progression opportunities you are most motivated to explore further. They are exciting and meaningful for you, which means they are likely to be a good fit for your future. When Helen worked at Microsoft, she was exploring a number of different progression possibilities and lots of them felt exciting, which made making a decision about what to do next difficult. It was only when she thought about which of her possibilities were most meaningful that her priorities become clear. This increased her confidence in the career decision she made, which ultimately resulted in her pivoting her career to grow our business (a decision she has never regretted!).

Shiny objects = don't get distracted

Shiny objects like promotions or qualifications can seem very appealing, and people invest a lot of time and attention in achieving them. However, they are only a small part of how you progress in your career and have a lower fit with what you find meaningful. Be careful not to overinvest in the pursuit of shiny objects as they are unlikely to be motivating to you in the medium and long term. A good example of this is a friend of Sarah's who turned down a 'shiny' promotion that didn't give her meaning in favour of a role that broadened her experience. She was still motivated by the possibility of promotion but had the confidence it would follow at some point in the future – just a bit later (which it did).

Stop = no action

These progression opportunities might have been inspired by what other people have done or what you feel like you should do, but they don't feel right for you. Sarah was once offered a sideways job move that was positioned as a fast track to achieving a director position. It would have been easy to say yes, but she wasn't excited about the role and it didn't fit well with what she found meaningful about progression (as we discussed in the introduction, it felt like progression for progression's sake) so she explored a different direction that would result in 'slower' but better progression for her.

Hard to do's = explore further

These opportunities fit well with what you find meaningful about progressing but perhaps they feel intimidating or hard in some sense, which gets in the way of feeling excited. With some effort in exploring and overcoming barriers, a 'hard to do' possibility can become a 'priority' over time. A good example of this is someone Helen coached who had a passion for working in sustainability but was currently in a very different role. She could see where she wanted to be but was feeling increasingly frustrated by how far away it felt. Together, they worked on a plan for her to get closer to her progression possibility by changing her network, volunteering and increasing her profile in the new area. The more actions she took, the more excited she found herself becoming about the progression possibility. This reinforced the feeling that her extra hard work was worth the effort as she was heading in the right direction for her.

Before we move on to Part 2 of the chapter, write down your two progression priorities below:

My progression priorities are:

1. _____

   _____

2. _____

   _____

PART 2: Prototyping

In the second part of this chapter, we focus on how you can start taking action on your progression priorities. We'll explore how prototyping will help you to test, learn and think creatively about how to achieve the progression you're motivated by. We then move on to how to coach yourself to secure the support you need to make your progression happen.

> *If a picture is worth a thousand words,*
> *a prototype is worth a thousand meetings.*
>
> **IDEO**

Borrowing the concept of prototyping from design and engineering is useful when we don't know all the answers or can't see the perfect solution in front of us. Prototyping is how you test and learn along the way, and, as Margaret Heffernan suggests in her book *Uncharted*, in an always changing world we all need to practise prototyping the future we want to create.

For this exercise it's useful to have some Post-it notes at the ready, or you could try using an online equivalent like Miro or Mural. As you prototype your progression, it's important to consider why that progression possibility is important to you. When you think about your *why* as well as your *what* you will generate more ideas. All ideas are valuable, even if some get you closer to what you want than others. On the next few pages we've included a couple of examples of how to prototype your progression priorities and then included a blank example so you can practise by scribbling in this book.

There are three steps to the process:

Step 1: What – write down your progression priority.
Step 2: Why – write down why that progression is important to you.
Step 3: How – write down all the ways you could prototype your progression.

Prototype your progression example 1: becoming a manager

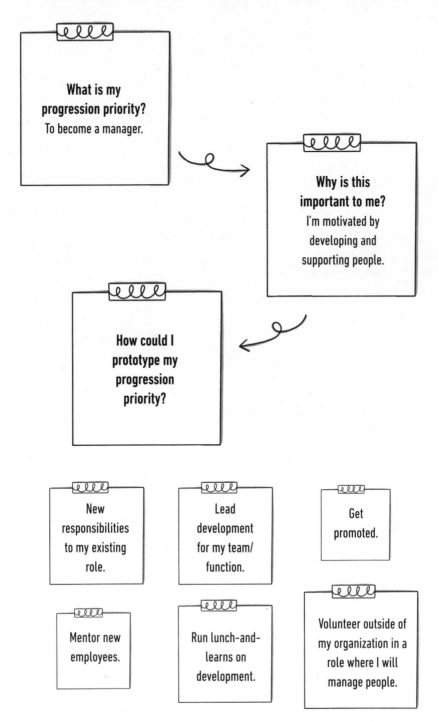

What is my progression priority?
To become a manager.

Why is this important to me?
I'm motivated by developing and supporting people.

How could I prototype my progression priority?

New responsibilities to my existing role.

Lead development for my team/ function.

Get promoted.

Mentor new employees.

Run lunch-and-learns on development.

Volunteer outside of my organization in a role where I will manage people.

Prototype your progression example 2: working a four-day week

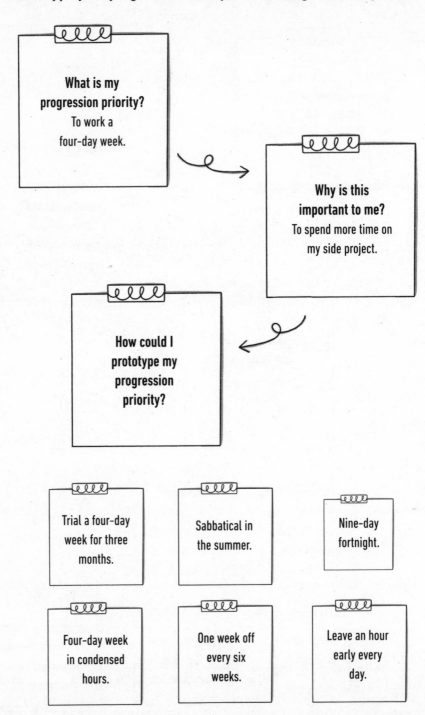

Prototype your progression

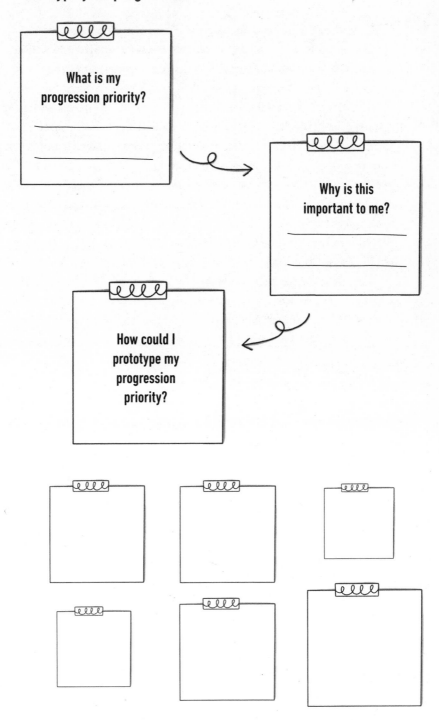

Securing support

The support of other people is a critical part of making progression happen. Support can show up in various ways: a manager advocating on your behalf, your partner agreeing to look after the kids so you can study, or maybe finding someone you want to do a job share with. The more specific you can be about the support you need, the more meaningful you can make your ask. It's also helpful to consider the reason someone might want to support you. Thinking about how they could also benefit from your progression makes it easier to be empathetic in your ask and overcome any objections. For your manager, your progression could bring new knowledge and skills into the team. For your mentors, it might give them a sense of pride that they have helped you achieve your ambitions. For your partner, it might be about your happiness or the work–life fit you'll achieve as a result.

Start by using the table below to think about the people you will need support from, how they can support you and why they will be motivated to give you the support you need.

My progression priority Example: to make a sideways move from Marketing to Sales		
Who I need support from	**How they can support me**	**Why they would want to give me their support**
Example: manager	Example: introduce me to their peer in Sales	Example: improves cross-functional relationships

We've shared three different ideas for action so you can secure the support you need to progress.

Idea for action: involve don't solve

You don't need to come up with all the answers to how you're going to make your progression happen on your own. If you involve the people you need support from in the prototyping process they will feel more included and engaged in your progression. They also might have new ideas you're not aware of or be able to introduce you to other people who can also offer their support.

Idea for action: your commitment creates commitment in others

You will receive more support if you can demonstrate you are committed to your own progress. If you have already started exploring and taking small steps on your progression it shows people that you are using their support to fill in gaps in your knowledge and expertise rather than asking them to do the hard work for you.

Idea for action: responding to rejection

Sometimes your progression isn't possible in the way you'd hoped for. You don't get the promotion you apply for, the funding you need for a course, the secondment you were excited about or the support to redesign your role to better fit your strengths. This happens to all of us, for example every time Sarah has applied for a promotion in her career, she didn't succeed the first time round.

If your progression doesn't go to plan, ask yourself the three coach yourself questions on the next page:

CY? What have I learnt from 'no'?

_____

_____

CY? How could I explore my progression priority in different ways that would still give me energy and meaning?

_____

_____

CY? Who might be able to support me to uncover new ways to prototype my progression that I haven't considered before?

_____

_____

If your progression doesn't happen in the way you'd hoped, you don't necessarily need to start again with a new priority. It might just take longer to achieve. Or you could find a different way to get there, and our expert below will help you explore what that might look like. You might choose to pause one priority in favour of concentrating your efforts on another area of progression until the time feels right to revisit it. The pursuit of a progression priority is never time wasted, it is time spent practising a skill that will be useful for the rest of your career.

Ask our expert: Adam Morgan, co-founder of eatbigfish and author of *A Beautiful Constraint*

Constraints can be beautiful. Instead of seeing them as unwelcome restrictions, we can choose to use them as an impetus to explore something new and arrive at breakthrough – not in spite of the constraint, but because of it.

Coaching question: *I'm keen to progress to a more senior role in my organization but there are no opportunities, so I feel I have no choice other than to leave (which I don't really want to do). I'm not sure what to do next. What would you advise?*

Expert answer: This is a constraint that many of us will experience at some point during our careers: the tricky dilemma of whether to stick or twist in pursuit of progression. When faced with a constraint we experience three types of response:

1. Victim: where we lower our ambition in response to a constraint.
2. Neutralizer: our ambition stays the same, but we find a different way to get there.
3. Transformer: we use our constraint as an impetus to step back and rethink the potential opportunity here, and maybe even increase our ambition for the quality of the outcome.

What's interesting about these three responses is that they represent not three different types of people but three *stages* that even the most talented and experienced problem solvers go through. Everyone starts in victim, and we should recognize that it's natural to initially find ourselves there. But we all have the potential to go from victim to transformer if we approach constraints with a *stubbornly adaptive* mindset and the *can-if* method to making progress.

Stubbornly adaptive mindset

People who are particularly good at turning constraints into possibilities are *stubbornly adaptive*. This means they know what to hold on to and when to let go. If your progression priority is about getting promoted, you are likely to be faced with a scenario of 'not now' rather than 'not ever'. The challenge is more one of an *enforced wait*. In this scenario we need to decide whether our objective is worth the wait, and I would challenge you even further to consider how could you make this 'wait' the best thing that has ever happened to you (in your career!) – how you can really make this constraint beautiful.

Can-if method

'Can-if' is a technique created by Colin Kelly: it means that when thinking about potential solutions to a challenge, however difficult, you don't allow yourself (or anyone else) to start a sentence 'I can't do that because . . .'; you have to start the sentence 'I can do that if . . .' Can-if statements help you to stay optimistic and open when faced with constraints. They steer you away from can't and a fixed view of the world that sees barriers and obstacles (*I can't because*) into a positive, possibility-based perspective that looks for opportunity, however unexpected (*I can if*). The solutions that can-if creates often generate unexpected benefits that wouldn't have come to you if the constraint hadn't presented itself. Here are some examples of how this might work for this specific scenario of progressing into a senior role:

   ✐ I can progress here if I design my own shadowing programme to learn from as many senior people in and out of my business as possible (who might also become my sponsors).

The unexpected benefit: by the time I am promoted I will have stronger relationships and a stronger support network in my new role.

   ✐ I can progress here if I think of this time as an opportunity to practise my leadership skills while in a job I feel confident about.

The unexpected benefit: by the time I am promoted I will be more confident and effective – and perhaps less stressed – in my new role.

   ✐ I can progress here if I introduce the idea of stretch roles, which could include going to work at one of our customers or suppliers for a year.

The unexpected benefit: by the time I am promoted I will have more authority and understanding in my new role.

In each of these *I can if . . .* examples the 'waiting' time could result not only in a senior role in the future, but an opportunity with more influence and impact than you originally anticipated. If you approach career constraints with the right mindset and method, you might find yourself making even more progress subsequently than you'd initially bargained for. Good luck – looking for the opportunities in constraints isn't always easy, but it's a question of nurture, not nature: I'm confident it's something that with practice we can all learn to do.

You COACH You

You can use the COACH tool to bring together your thoughts and reflections from this chapter and apply them to the specific career challenge you might be facing at the moment. Taking the time to bring your insights together using COACH will help you to be clear about your actions, increase your confidence and spot the support you need. The more you practise using COACH, the more you'll find yourself using it for lots of different challenges both at work and in your career.

COACH

Clarity – what is your coaching challenge?

Options – what options could you explore?

Action – what actions will you take?

Confidence – how confident are you about taking those actions?

Help – what help do you need to overcome your challenge?

Summary

Progression: Moving forward with momentum.

We keep moving forward because we're curious and curiosity keeps leading us down new paths.
Walt Disney

Why coach yourself?

Being proactive about your progression will increase your options and opportunities.

Taking ownership of your progression increases the control you have in your career and makes your development less dependent on other people.

Coach yourself concepts

Progression possibilities: Identifying and exploring different directions and ways in which you could progress in your career.

Progression prototyping: Taking a test-and-learn approach to explore the possibilities that feel motivating for you.

COACHING TOOLS

Progression possibilities

Prioritizing progression

Progression prototyping

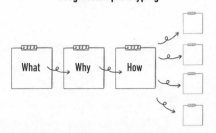

COACH YOURSELF QUESTIONS

1. Why is progression motivating to me?
2. What are all the options for progression I could explore?
3. How can I signal the support that I need to progress to other people?
4. How can my constraints be used to my advantage?
5. What's one action I could take this week to start making progress?

Listen	Free downloads
Squiggly Careers podcast #217 with Sophie Williams	www.amazingif.com

Action may not always bring happiness: but there is no happiness without action.

BENJAMIN
DISRAELI

I truly believe that each of us must find meaning in our work. The best work happens when you know that it's not just work but something that will improve other people's lives.

SATYA
NADELLA

7 ⟿ Purpose

How you develop a sense of direction and do meaningful work

Purpose: why coach yourself

1. Finding purpose in our work increases the long-term sense of satisfaction we feel in our lives and improves how engaged and effective we are in our jobs today.
2. In the twists and turns of a squiggly career our purpose gives us a sense of direction and something meaningful to make progress towards.

Finding purpose from our work

We find purpose from many places: our relationships, hobbies, career, health and faith. When we have a sense of purpose in our lives our overall health improves, and we even live for longer, on average.[38] When asked what makes life meaningful, a US study found that, after family, career was the next most important contributor.[39] For most of us, work is a significant source of meaning and a big part of who we are.

In his book *Alive at Work*, Daniel Cable describes the positive relationship between being purposeful in our work and feeling happier in our lives. In particular, researchers have found that doing work where we

> *Happiness does not come from doing easy work but from the afterglow of satisfaction that comes after the achievement of a difficult task that demanded our best.*
>
> **THEODORE RUBIN**

are making progress towards our purpose contributes to *eudemonic happiness*. This is the long-term sense of satisfaction we feel from 'a life well led'. The positive impact of purposeful work also shows up in the day-to-day experience of doing our jobs. McKinsey research in 2020 found that people who are living their purpose at work are more likely to sustain and improve their effectiveness, are four times more engaged in their work and have five times higher well-being than those who are not.[40]

Coaching yourself to find your purpose at work doesn't mean that every day will be easy, or even enjoyable, but it does mean that the hard work, inevitable stresses and compromises along the way will feel worth it.

A sense of direction

Though the more spontaneous amongst us might feel comfortable living by the mantra on Sarah's luggage tag, our careers are too important to leave to chance. We interview lots of inspiring people for our podcast and books and it's not uncommon to hear them say they had no career plan and even express surprise at where

> *Does anyone know where we're going? No – but I hope it's nice when we get there.*
>
> **SARAH'S LUGGAGE TAG**

they've ended up. However, what we've noticed is that when you dig a bit deeper all these people have one thing in common: a sense of direction that has helped to guide their career. This direction has prompted decisions about where to go and what to do (and not do) next. It also helps them to respond to the inevitable wrong turns along the way, and means that they are doing work that is meaningful to them.

What is purpose?

The concept of purpose has become popular for both individuals and organizations over the past few years. This has led to some, in our view, unhelpful interpretations of what purpose means, from the clichéd career

advice of *do what you love* to organizations adopting
superficial purpose statements. Purpose is not words
on an office wall or a shiny screensaver. Purpose is
your North Star. It guides your decisions and gives
you confidence in where you're going. The best
reasons for spending time exploring your purpose are
practical ones. You will make better decisions about
your career, spend more time every day doing work that
matters to you and feel more fulfilled now and in the future.

There is no single blueprint for a meaningful career.

ROMAN KRZNARIC

Purpose principles

We define purpose as having a sense of direction in your career and doing
work you find meaningful. There are three purpose principles that are
useful to consider, and one watch-out to be aware of, as you start coaching
yourself through this chapter:

1. A direction, not a destination.
2. An ambition, not an answer.
3. A work-in-progress, not the pursuit of perfection.

*To explore without always reaching a destination;
to search without necessarily finding an answer; to
get lost in the journey for the journey's sake.*

CLARISSA SEBAG-MONTEFIORE

A direction not a destination

Purpose is not something you can tick off your to-do list and there is never
a moment when you will be able to say 'My work here is done'. Your
purpose is a direction you head towards rather than a destination you
reach.

226   YOU COACH YOU

An ambition not an answer

Your purpose is an ambition, not something you need to be able to answer or achieve. You don't need to be limited by where you are today or what you've achieved in the past.

Work-in-progress not perfection

There is no such thing as a perfect purpose and your direction is likely to change as you have different career experiences and increase your self-awareness. We don't need to put pressure on ourselves to have an 'a-ha' moment when the clouds clear and your purpose emerges fully formed in a lightning bolt of inspiration. Your purpose will always feel more work-in-progress than perfect.

There is no finish line.

NIKE

Watch-out – purpose anxiety

The search for purpose can lead to what researcher Larissa Rainey describes as 'purpose anxiety'. This anxiety can be experienced at two different stages, either when you're struggling to uncover what your purpose is or when trying to live your purpose (both topics we're going to cover in this chapter). This anxiety can show up as feelings of stress, worry, frustration or fear. In Rainey's research 91 per cent of participants shared that they had experienced purpose anxiety at some point in their life.[41] As you coach yourself through finding and living your purpose at work be aware of how you're feeling. If you experience some anxiety, know that this is a common part of the process and it could be a good time to press pause for a few days, or it might be a useful prompt to have a conversation with one of your mentors (an idea for action we cover in Part 2 of this chapter).

Start by letting go of the idea of 'finding' your purpose. It is not in Lost Property somewhere, it is in your consciousness, so the first step is to listen to the moments that bring you the most joy, comfort and ease. That is where the core of your purpose resides.

When you connect with these moments and feelings, ask yourself, Where am I? Who am I with? What am I doing/saying? Now, write them down and look for the common parts. Your purpose will become clearer the more you listen and refine the list.

NATALIE
CAMPBELL

Thinking traps and positive prompts

Thinking traps are a useful way to identify any assumptions you have that could get in the way of being open and optimistic in your coaching approach.

〰 *My purpose doesn't fit with my organization.*
〰 *I can't earn enough money and have purpose at work.*
〰 *To have purpose I need to work for a charity or good cause.*
〰 *It's too late for me to change direction towards something more purposeful.*
〰 *I go to work for a pay-slip; I don't need purpose at work.*

Reframing your thinking traps as positive prompts will unlock your assumptions and give you the ability to explore options and possibilities as you coach yourself.

From: My purpose doesn't fit with my organization.
To: What other opportunities (side projects, volunteering, causes) could I explore outside my organization to make progress towards my purpose?

From: I can't earn enough money and have purpose at work.
To: Who has been able to combine earning 'enough' with having purpose at work?

From: To have purpose I need to work for a charity or good cause.
To: Apart from charities and philanthropists, which organizations and individuals have a positive impact on the world?

From: It's too late for me to change direction towards something more purposeful.
To: What are the small steps I could take now that would make my work more meaningful?

From: I go to work for a pay-slip; I don't need purpose at work.
To: If I could add purpose to my pay-slip what benefits might I gain?

My purpose thinking trap

_____

My purpose positive prompt

_____

How to coach yourself on purpose

This section of the chapter is where we want you to get practical about your purpose. We will support you to understand what direction feels motivating for your career and how to do more meaningful work.

In Part 1 we cover:

ℒ↗ *How to explore your purpose using different mind-map tools.*
ℒ↗ *How to create your work-in-progress purpose statement.*

In Part 2 we focus on:

ℒ↗ *How to identify your meaning at work today using our meaning meter.*
ℒ↗ *How to maximize your moments of meaning by using your strengths, finding your purpose fit and increasing your positive people impact.*

The chapter has a final exercise called You Create You to bring all your insights together. We finish with our expert Dan Cable, London Business School professor, who tells us why following your blisters is more useful advice than following your passions when it comes to finding our purpose.

PART 1: Exploring my purpose

Purpose mind-map

Most of us haven't spent much time thinking about our purpose, so this exercise is designed to get you started. Use the mind-map opposite to jot down your answers to each of the questions. We'd suggest doing this exercise at least twice. If you have time now, scribble down the first thoughts that come to mind in response to each question. These are all 'big' questions that you will need time to think through properly. If you can, keep your mind-map somewhere you can see it regularly for the next few weeks so you can continue to capture new thoughts and insights that spring to mind. It's amazing the difference it can make even doing this exercise twice in one day.

Purpose mind-map

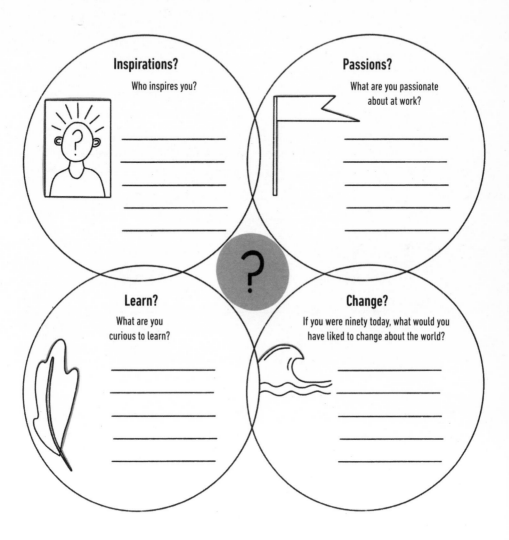

Now you've completed your mind-map ask yourself the following two coach yourself questions:

CY? How did thinking about my purpose make me feel?

_____

CY? What do I notice about my answers?

_____

Now revisit each of the answers in your mind-map and ask yourself a 'why' coach yourself question, for example:

CY? Why does that matter to me?

_____

At this point you might be able to see some consistent themes in your reflections or you might feel stuck and believe your mind-map represents a random collection of words that don't add up to much (yet). Don't panic if you're struggling at this stage; these are not easy questions to answer. To think about your purpose from a different perspective, work through the next two ideas for action.

Idea for action: your pessimistic purpose

Rather than asking yourself lots of questions about what your purpose is, it can be easier to start with what it _isn't_. To do this, ask yourself the following coach yourself questions:

CY? What gets me frustrated about the work that I do?

_____

CY? Who makes me angry?

_____

CY? Which areas of my work am I bored by?

_____

CY? Fast-forward to the future and I'm ninety years old. What has stayed the same about the world that makes me most disappointed?

_____

It can be cathartic to discover some clarity about your purpose by exploring the areas that feel purposeless to you. Now you have some sense of what finding your purpose doesn't look like, try repeating the purpose mind-map exercise again to see if you have any new insights to note down.

Idea for action: guess what?

It's useful to take a break from thinking about ourselves and spend some time in other people's worlds. This is a fun and inspiring exercise that encourages you to think about what someone else's purpose might be. At the same time, you'll probably find it helps you to develop your own thoughts further. There are three simple steps to playing 'guess what?':

1. Pick five people who inspire you and who share their work publicly.
2. Spend some time reading, watching and listening to their work.
3. Imagine (or even write down) what their purpose mind-map might look like.

If you need some help to get started, here is a list of five people we're inspired by:

1. Brené Brown
2. Indra Nooyi
3. Jacinda Ardern
4. Marcus Rashford
5. Grayson Perry

Work-in-progress purpose statements

We now want to use your mind-map to create your work-in-progress purpose statements. Your aim at this point is not to craft the perfect purpose statement but to experiment with lots of different statements to see what feels most motivating and memorable to you. To get started, try completing each of the sentences below:

I go to work to

_____

What matters to me about my work is

_____

When I go to bed I feel happy about my day if

_____

A tweet to describe why I go to work would say

_____

And here are a few examples of work-in-progress purpose statements from people who've had a go at this exercise in our workshops.

- 'Solving problems that positively impact lots of people' – Rob George, customer and online director, McColl's.
- 'Helping someone to feel their best' – Katherine Ellis, owner, Reflections Beauty Therapy.

⤳ 'To inspire and bring about change, one person at a time.' – Dominique Bergiers, learning and development manager, Levi Strauss & Co.

My work-in-progress purpose statement

_____

We recommend that you continue to revisit Part 1 of this chapter at relevant points throughout your career. In Part 2 we move our focus onto how you can make progress towards your purpose and do more meaningful work.

PART 2 – Making progress towards your purpose

To make progress towards your purpose we need to connect *why* you go to work with *what* you spend your days doing. Knowing the direction we want to head in without making progress towards it leaves us feeling at best frustrated and at worst demotivated. In Part 2 we're going to support you to coach yourself in three ways:

> *Make your work to be in keeping with your purpose.*
>
> **LEONARDO DA VINCI**

1. Identify how meaningful your work is today.
2. Consider how you can find more moments of meaning in your work.
3. Assess the fit between your purpose and your organization.

Your meaning meter

Work is rarely 100 per cent meaningful or 100 per cent meaningless. Most of us are somewhere between these two points on a spectrum. Start by intuitively identifying where you are on the meaningless to meaningful scale today.

How meaningful does your work today feel on a scale of 0 to 100 per cent?

0 PER CENT   100 PER CENT

Now consider these two coach yourself questions:

CY? What aspect of my work at the moment do I find most meaningful?

_____

CY? What aspect of my work at the moment do I find least meaningful?

_____

Idea for action: track your meaningful moments

You could also do the exercise above at the end of each day for a week or a month. This would help you to track how much your scale varies and identify specifically what contributes to your scale moving up or down. Wherever you are on the meaning meter, we all have room for improvement. The next exercise will help you to consider how you can maximize moments of meaning in your job today.

Maximize your moments of meaning

To increase how meaningful your work is there are three connected areas you can coach yourself on:

1. Using your strengths in pursuit of your purpose (your what).
2. Finding your purpose fit (your where).
3. Understanding your positive people impact (your who).

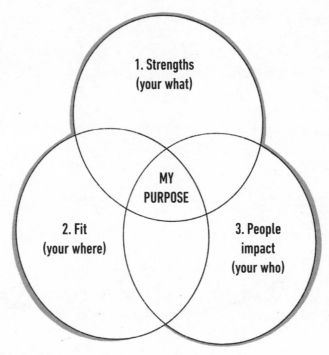

Your strengths

Your strengths are you at your best. They're the things that you're great at and that give you energy. They can be anything from listening to coding, problem solving to copywriting. When you know what your strengths are and use them in pursuit of your purpose, your work will feel motivating and meaningful. To start surfacing your strengths and understand how much you're using them work through the strengths spotlight and fuel your frequency exercises below.

1. Strengths spotlight

Reflecting on your work over the last few months, note down three examples of times where one or more of your strengths have been in the spotlight. These spotlight moments are likely to be when you were enjoying your work and your strengths were standing out. Describe these spotlight moments in as much detail as you can – who were you working with, what were you working on, where were you working?

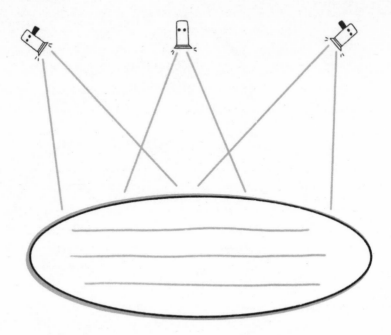

If at this point you're feeling a bit stuck on identifying your strengths, we'd recommend listening to our *Squiggly Careers* podcast episodes 27 ('Finding Out Your Strengths') and 122 ('How to Make Your Strengths Stand Out').

Fuel your frequency

Complete the table below to reflect on how much you are using your strengths to make progress towards your purpose in your role today.

Connecting your purpose and your strengths	
My work-in-progress purpose:	
Three of my strengths	How often do I use each strength in pursuit of my purpose (daily, weekly, monthly, occasionally, never)
1.	
2.	
3.	

You can now use your insights from the above exercise to identify ways you can fuel your frequency. For example, if you're currently using your strength occasionally how could you move that to monthly? If you're at never, how could you get to occasionally? Below we have shared an idea for action that will support you to use your strengths more frequently to make progress towards your purpose.

Idea for action: find your meaning mentors

A meaning mentor combines three things: an understanding of your purpose, insight into your strengths and the ability to spot and connect you with opportunities to make progress. When you feel disconnected from your purpose or lost about what to do next, a meaning mentor can help to show you the art of the possible and inspire you to take action.

An example of a meaning mentor is Sarah's relationship with Sherilyn Shackell, founder and CEO of The Marketing Academy. When Sarah started to explore her work-in-progress purpose about helping people with their careers, it felt daunting and she was stuck about where to start. She asked Sherilyn for advice on how to move forward. Sherilyn made a great meaning mentor because she knew Sarah and her strengths well, shared a passion for supporting people to develop and had a strong network Sarah could learn from. Over the years Sherilyn generously gave her time and her connections to help Sarah and, as a result, Sarah was able to find more opportunities to use her strengths in pursuit of her purpose and increase how meaningful her work felt.

To find your own meaning mentor, think about the people who:

  know your strengths,
  understand your purpose,
  can help you make progress towards your purpose.

They might include past managers, people you have met through your networks or colleagues you've felt a sense of connection with. Ask those people for their thoughts and ideas on how you can use your strengths to help to move forward with your purpose. If asking for help feels hard, try reading our expert section in the resilience chapter (p. 67), where Kajal Odedra, director of Change.org shares some words of wisdom on the art of asking and the importance of mentors.

2. Find your purpose fit

Your purpose won't be exactly the same as the purpose of your organization, even if the company belongs to you. However, when there is a close connection between the direction you're heading in and where your organization wants to go, you are more likely to make progress towards your purpose at work.

Five questions to find your fit

To get a sense of you and your organization's purpose fit, complete the questionnaire below. The answers will help you to identify where you have gaps today and the coach yourself questions will support you to fill those gaps. These questions are also helpful to come back to when making decisions about future roles as this will prompt you to include purpose fit as part of your decision criteria.

What's your purpose fit?

Question 1: do you know the purpose of your organization?

> **A:** No
> **B:** Sort of
> **C:** Yes

Question 2: Which of these four diagrams best reflects the sense of connection you feel with your organization's purpose.

> **A:** No overlap
> **B:** Some overlap
> **C:** Moderate overlap
> **D:** Nearly as one

Question 3: How much of yourself do you bring to work every day?

A: Very little (less than 10 per cent)
B: Not very much (10–30 per cent)
C: It varies (30–60 per cent)
D: Most of me (60–90 per cent)
E: I'm me pretty much all the time (90 per cent +)

Question 4: How would you feel if your organization didn't exist tomorrow?

A: Saw it coming and feel fine
B: Concerned for myself and my colleagues but not surprised
C: Shocked and sad – I think what we do has a positive impact
D: Would try to find a way to continue the work because it matters so much to me

Question 5: You get offered the opportunity to own part of your organization, how do you react?

A: No thanks
B: Maybe, but only if some of my concerns are addressed
C: I have some questions, but I'll definitely consider it
D: Yes please, where do I sign?

Interpreting your score

A – 0	B – 1	C – 2	D – 3	E – 4

Total score: . . . .

0–4: Tough times. Your scores suggest you don't feel connected to your organization, and this might mean it's time to think about making a change.

> **CY?** What can I start or join outside my day job that will give me the opportunity to make progress on my purpose (volunteering, side-projects, hobbies, campaigning)?

5–8: Room for improvement. You feel some limited sense of connection to your organization but there's lots of opportunities for improvement.

> **CY?** How could I learn more about my organization's purpose? (What curious conversations could I have? Which teams could I spend time with? What could I read?)

9–12: Positive progress. You have a positive connection with your organization but there are definitely opportunities to strengthen that connection.

> **CY?** Who could I build relationships with in my organization who could be potential meaning mentors (reminder: see previous exercise)?

13+: Nearly flawless fit. Brilliant! There is a strong connection between your why and why your organization exists.

> **CY?** How could I support other people to make the same strong connection that I have? (This might be supporting my team, organization or industry.)

3. Your positive people impact

Helper's high

By helping other people, we help
ourselves. Every time we help someone,
however small that help might be, we
benefit from something psychologists
call 'helper's high'. This is the natural,
uplifting high we get from giving and
kindness, as after doing something good our
bodies release feel-good endorphins that reward

> *Giving back is as good for you as it is for those you are helping, because giving gives you purpose. When you have a purpose-driven life, you're a happier person.*
>
> **GOLDIE HAWN**

us for our actions. Through our work we all have the opportunity to help,
and have a positive impact on other people. Sometimes we've just lost
sight of our impact, or need to consider it more intentionally. It's also
important to recognize that helping others is not the same as being selfless.
As Adam Grant points out in his book *Give and Take*, the most successful
givers are those who are willing to give more than they receive, but
without forgetting their own interests. The next few coaching exercises
will help you do two things:

1. Recognize your positive people impact today.
2. Identify how you could increase your people impact to make
   progress on your purpose.

Your positive people impact today

We want to start by supporting you to be aware of and appreciate the
positive impact you have on other people at the moment.

1. Look back over your week and list the five people you spend the
   most time with (use the table on the next page).
2. For each person rate whether you feel your positive impact on them
   is high, medium or low.
3. Note down any examples of how your positive impact shows up
   with each person.
4. Answer the coach yourself questions in the table to reflect on where
   you are having the most and least impact.

My positive people impact today		
The five people I spend the most time with	My impact today (high, medium, low)	How does my impact show up?
Example: Bryony	Example: Medium	Example: helping her to troubleshoot/solve any problems that crop up during the week
1)		
2)		
3)		
4)		
5)		

CY? Who do I have the most positive impact on and why?

_____

CY? Who do I have the least positive impact on and why?

_____

CY? Where can I spot opportunities to increase my impact?

_____

Idea for action: impact insights

This idea for action will help you to understand other people's perceptions of the impact you make. You might be surprised that you're having more impact with some people than you're giving yourself credit for. Or maybe you thought your positive impact would be about the work you produce but it's more about one of your behaviours – your listening skills, for example. You can gather these insights in whatever way works for you; it can be informal over a cup of tea or an instant message, especially if you already have a good relationship with someone. If you want to be more structured in your approach, there are a couple of examples below of how you could ask for impact insights.

To someone you work with: *We've been working together on this project for a while now and I'm keen to know how I'm doing. Could you share with me where you think I have the most positive impact on the project?*

To your manager: *What is your perspective on when you think I have a positive impact on other members of our team?*

Connecting the dots between your purpose and your people

Increasing your positive impact with the people you already know and through the work you already do is usually the easiest way to start increasing your moments of meaning. However, depending on how strong the fit is between you and your organization's purpose this may or may not help you to make progress towards your purpose. This next exercise is designed to connect the two concepts we've been exploring together: your positive people impact and making progress towards your purpose.

Use the diagram on the next page to consider the different places and people you could support and spend time with that are connected to your work-in-progress purpose. If you're not sure how you could support and offer help to a group, don't let this hold you back. We often discover the help that people need only once we get to know them. As long as you bring a 'giving mindset' to a group you can feel confident that you will find a way to make a positive impact on other people. We've made a few suggestions to get you started and left some circles blank for your ideas too.

Connect the dots between your work-in-progress purpose and positive people impact

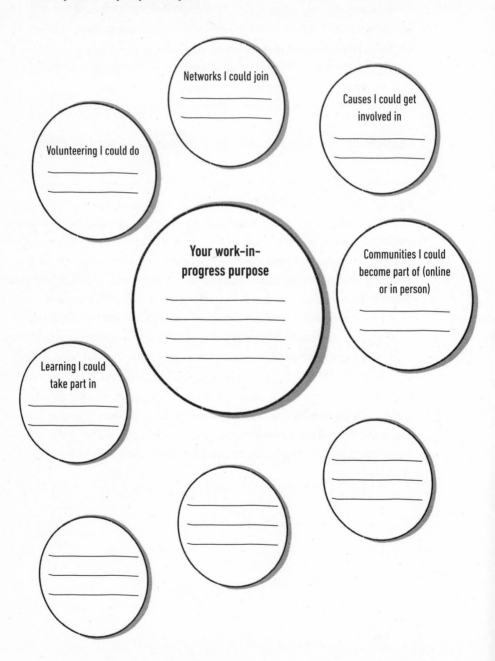

Now reflect on your connected dots and answer the following coach yourself questions to work out what next.

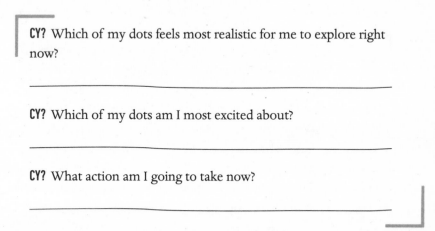

CY? Which of my dots feels most realistic for me to explore right now?

_____

CY? Which of my dots am I most excited about?

_____

CY? What action am I going to take now?

_____

In Part 2 of this chapter, you have coached yourself on how meaningful your work is today and how you can maximize your moments of meaning through using your strengths (your what), fit with your organization (your where) and your people impact (your who). We now have one final exercise, You Create You, to support you to reflect on all your insights and actions on purpose so far and put them together in one place.

You Create You

This final exercise is designed to bring together your insights on the direction you're motivated by and the work you find meaningful. It's a bit like creating an imaginary job role but rather than starting with an organization and what a role needs, this starts with you and how you can be at your best. The You Create You profile might feel out of reach right now, but there is a lot of power in using pen and paper to commit to what your work could look like. It helps us to focus on finding opportunities and taking actions to get one step closer to making it a reality. After completing this exercise, make a note in your calendar to come back to it in six months' time to see what progress you've made. You'll either be surprised by how far you've come or, if nothing has changed, it will be a useful prompt to consider what you might want to do differently.

You Create You: _____
(your name)

Job title: _____
(it doesn't need to exist today)

I come to work to _____
(choose your favourite work-in-progress purpose statement)

I have a reputation for _____
(my strengths)

I spend my days _____
(describe your most meaningful work)

I'm inspired by _____
(people, places, organizations, networks)

I'm most proud of _____
(what would you like to be true about the work that you do?)

I have a positive impact on _____
(describe the people that you have a positive impact on)

Even if you don't believe you have a 'purpose' think about the work you can do in the world that would make a difference to others. What art can you make, what comfort can you bring, what wrong can you set right? If you can do it, you should do it.

MAGGIE
SMITH

Ask our expert: Dan Cable, London Business School professor and author of *Alive at Work*

If you're looking to find a career that will matter to you, instead of looking only in the direction of 'passion', also think about the activities that you return to – despite the fact that they are harder to complete than things you are more immediately or emotionally drawn to.

Coaching question: *I want to find a career that feels purposeful, but I feel stuck. How do I get started?*

Expert answer: The go-to answer to finding purpose in your career is *follow your passion*.[42] But for many of us, me included, this feels too glib to be useful. Even worse, this kind of advice can be damaging when we start to beat ourselves up if we don't find ourselves in our dream job or living our best life day in, day out. Instead of the bumper-sticker style advice of 'follow your bliss' or 'do what you love' my suggestion, based on studying people's job choices and career successes for twenty-five years, is *follow your blisters*.

Follow your blisters
A blister appears when something wears at you – and even chafes you a bit – but you keep getting drawn back to it. What I like about the phrase is that it implies something about perseverance and struggling through tasks even though they are not always blissful. 'Follow your blisters' makes me ask myself the question, *What kind of work do I find myself coming back to again and again, even when I don't succeed right away, when it seems like it's taking too long to make progress, or when I get discouraged?* So, if you're looking to find a career that will matter to you, instead of looking only in the direction of 'passion', also think about the activities that you return to – despite the fact that they are harder to complete than things you are more immediately or emotionally drawn to.

What do you never need to put on your to-do list?
Martin Seligman, one of the parents of positive psychology, asks the question this way: 'What activities were you already doing as a child that you still like to do now?' What activities do you never need to put on your to-do list? You may notice that other people need to remind themselves to analyse the metrics of their social media posts

while you are naturally pulled towards cracking the code of what performs well. You may notice that other people dread or avoid giving presentations while you are up late doing research to support your points and practising in front of the mirror. Pay attention to this. And in comparison, also notice what tasks you have to nudge and remind yourself to complete at all. The things that always seem to get done often reveal insight into what will fulfil you in your career.

Develop your 'wabi-sabi'
Finally, 'follow your blisters' implies something that you come back to so many times that you eventually move past the blister stage, into toughened skin. Eventually, the activity 'marks you' through use and practice, and you develop a special competence. When you practise an activity a bit more obsessively than other people, you build unique character – you earn some wear and some healing that makes you idiosyncratic, and a little unbalanced. You develop what the Japanese might call 'wabi-sabi' – a beauty caused by the personalized texture you have earned and the places you are not quite symmetrical.

You COACH You

You can use the COACH tool to bring together your thoughts and reflections from this chapter and apply them to the specific career challenge you might be facing at the moment. Taking the time to bring your insights together using COACH will help you to be clear about your actions, increase your confidence and spot the support you need. The more you practise using COACH, the more you'll find yourself using it for lots of different challenges both at work and in your career.

COACH

Clarity – what is your coaching challenge?

Options – what options could you explore?

Action – what actions will you take?

Confidence – how confident are you about taking those actions?

Help – what help do you need to overcome your challenge?

Summary

Purpose: How you develop a sense of direction and do meaningful work.

*I truly believe that each of us must find meaning in our work. The best work happens when
you know that it's not just work but something that will improve other people's lives.*
Satya Nadella

Why coach yourself?	Coach yourself concepts
Finding purpose in your work will increase the long-term sense of satisfaction you feel in your life and improve your job effectiveness and engagement.	**Work-in-progress purpose statements:** A motivating and memorable way for you to describe the direction you're heading towards in your career.
In the twists and turns of a squiggly career your purpose gives you a sense of direction and something meaningful to make progress towards.	**Meaning meter:** A way to get an 'at-a-glance' measure for how meaningful your work feels today.

COACHING TOOLS

Purpose mind-map	Maximize meaning
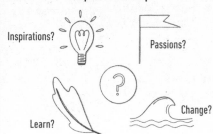	

Finding your fit

  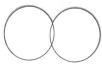

COACH YOURSELF QUESTIONS

1. What do I find most meaningful about my work?
2. How frequently am I using my strengths in my job today?
3. How would I describe the fit between what I care about and what matters to my organization?
4. What opportunities can I spot to increase my positive impact on other people?
5. I'm 90, what would I liked to have changed about the world?

Listen	Free downloads
Squiggly Careers podcast #213 with Dan Cable	www.amazingif.com

I believe people are in
our lives for a reason.
We're here to learn
from each other.

GILLIAN
ANDERSON

8 ✐⟶ Advice from All Areas

Career advice from all walks of life to inspire you

This chapter is a ready-made career community of incredible people offering you their words of wisdom especially for this book. A range of experts from all walks of life have generously agreed to share their career advice for us all to benefit from. You will learn from Olympians and creative pioneers, from campaigners and the people who looked after us during the pandemic. The one thing that everyone in this chapter has in common is that they are doing inspiring work that is making a positive difference. Collecting this career advice has been a pleasure and a privilege and we hope you find it as thought-provoking and inspiring as we have.

Just because you're good at something doesn't mean you have to do it.

> I was given this piece of advice when I was running tech companies and I was really getting to the point of thinking I don't know how much longer I can do this and everybody kept saying, 'But Margaret you're so good at it,' and that one sentence kind of set me free . . . if you're good at one thing then you're probably good at something else and if you're good at something but you don't enjoy it find something else.
>
> **MARGARET HEFFERNAN, ENTREPRENEUR, CEO, WRITER AND KEYNOTE SPEAKER**

Always fish upstream.

> My grandfather always used to say this to people, 'Always fish upstream', and he
> meant by that, think about the different and the unusual. It's not career advice, but
> I took that to heart. He was an entrepreneur and I've been lucky enough to be an
> entrepreneur. And to me fishing upstream means you don't always need to go with
> the tide and not worrying about it if you don't. There's a real strength in feeling your
> voice is the different, provocative, challenging one and though it can be hard, it can
> also really make you feel like you're achieving something.
>
> **MARTHA LANE FOX CBE, BRITISH BUSINESSWOMAN AND PHILANTHROPIST**

Collaborate to accelerate.

> I'm often saying collaborate to accelerate, we don't have to work alone, and alone
> can be very isolating, but if you have the right supportive networks that changes
> lives. And ABC – Always Be Curious.
>
> **KANYA KING CBE, FOUNDER OF MUSIC OF BLACK ORIGIN (MOBO) AWARDS**

Be you, be yourself, but be the best of you.

> **LEVI ROOTS, BRITISH-JAMAICAN REGGAE MUSICIAN, CHEF AND AUTHOR**

Make yourself useful.

> This may sound banal but I'm serious. Work out what your business needs and be
> the solution. A top LA agent once told me that, while she wasn't the smartest in the
> industry and she wasn't the most charming either, she made it her job to always
> respond to her clients personally, within minutes of them contacting her, because
> she understood that was the service they valued above all else. By focusing on being
> the most useful she could be, she rose to heights that would make most people's
> noses bleed. Not all jobs, business and client needs are as straightforward as that,
> but being the go-to person for solving problems is key to career progress as far as I
> am concerned.
>
> **ZOE COLLINS, CHIEF CONTENT OFFICER, JAMIE OLIVER GROUP**

Train yourself to trust yourself.

It's a skill, you have to train yourself to trust yourself. It's easy to default to someone else in the room or to follow someone else's lead. It's something I still work on and have to remind myself of, because with live television there is always a producer in your ear or on the floor, so it can become easy to just go along with things and ignore how you really feel. Not everything has to be instant, so even taking a few seconds to just allow yourself to feel and figure out what your instincts are telling you is worthwhile.

IAN WRIGHT MBE,
FORMER PROFESSIONAL
FOOTBALLER AND
TELEVISION AND RADIO
PERSONALITY

Ask yourself: what impact do I want to have?

> Instead of thinking about what kind of career you want, think about your own impact. What impact do you want to have?
>
> **HEATHER MCGREGOR CBE, EXECUTIVE DEAN, EDINBURGH BUSINESS SCHOOL**

Take time for yourself.

> I have suffered from anxiety for a long time and that's been a journey of discovery for me. I've done a lot of work on understanding myself and understanding what it is that made me feel certain ways. I know now that it's a culture of trust, a support network and taking time away that is most crucial for me and it's become an incredibly important part of managing myself.
>
> **BEN LEVINSON, HEAD TEACHER, KENSINGTON PRIMARY SCHOOL**

Am I supposed to be here right now?

> One thing that I try and take with me into every piece of work that I do, is 'Am I supposed to be here, right now?' I find it such a gratifying and thought-provoking sentiment, because, especially in the media industry and fashion industries respectively, they're fast paced and are heavily focused on progression. But asking myself if I am in fact supposed to be here, right now, allows me to really be honest with myself about whether or not I am rushing my career. It's important to do that for you, but also for others around you. Are you taking up space? How have you got to this position? Is it your position to be in? What this essentially is, is a self-appraisal every time you take on a new challenge and task in work. You have to be able to be completely honest with yourself whenever you work because when your work is your passion, you have to 100 per cent love and know that what you're doing in that moment is the right thing for *you*.
>
> **JAMIE WINDUST, CONTRIBUTING EDITOR, *GAY TIMES*, AUTHOR AND PRESENTER**

Own your failures with as much conviction as your success.

You will always learn more from the things you do wrong than the things you do right. When you own your failure, you're taking accountability.

DR SABRINA COHEN-HATTON, CHIEF FIRE OFFICER AT WEST SUSSEX FIRE AND RESCUE SERVICE

Be stubborn about the things you believe in.

> Bring yourself totally to everything you do and you won't go far wrong. Stand out. Be stubborn about things you believe in. Surround yourself with real, weird and wonderful characters with superpowers that complement your own. Make the things you love the things that pay you. Smile at everyone. Don't stress about career paths. Wear sequins to meetings. Take it from me: the thirty-seven-year-old pink-haired start-up founder/blogger/comedian/author with Parkinson's, failing neck muscles and hands that permanently quiver but who has never been happier or more fulfilled.

EMMA LAWTON, PARKINSON'S EDUCATOR, STAND-UP COMIC AND WRITER

The perfect job is hard to find; figure out what matters most right now.

> I have been most successful in my life so far when I have followed my heart and listened to my intuition. On a more practical note, if the perfect job is hard to find, try breaking down what you are looking for into function, industry and location. If you can start by ticking one or two of the boxes, that will move you in the right direction. It might take you a couple of career leaps to tick all three.

LAURA RUDOE, FOUNDER, EVOLVE BEAUTY

Being scared makes you sharper.

> Take chances early on – if someone offers you the opportunity to work on something you'd never considered but you think it will be interesting, do it. For me, it was reporting on mountain biking at the 1996 Olympics. I was there to cover the equestrian events (which I knew and understood) but the mountain biking came through the Horse Park so . . . Since then I've done darts, bowls, rugby league, winter sports – all sorts of things that have taken me out of my comfort zone and taught me things as a broadcaster. I enjoy feeling a bit scared and I think it makes me sharper. It's easy to stay safe but sometimes that can make you lazy. I'd rather take chances and try to push myself into different zones. That's why I write books – it's the scariest thing of all to try to create something worthwhile and interesting that will last long after I'm gone (or be recycled!).

CLARE BALDING, BROADCASTER, JOURNALIST AND AUTHOR

Being curiosity-led brings a kind of courage.

I have been told at key points in my life by people I really respected, an inspirational teacher, a university tutor and an older, wiser ambassador when I was in the Foreign Office, not to worry about the 'right' or 'wrong' career move, not to think about what I 'should' do, but to listen and tune in to my 'inner voice' and go where my curiosity took me. Being curiosity-led brings a kind of courage with it, permission to try something out, even if you're not sure if it will work out or not. That approach has certainly taken me on some amazing journeys.

CATH BISHOP,
FORMER BRITISH
ROWER, OLYMPIC
SILVER MEDALLIST

Work on the hardest problem.

> Every action in your life has led you to become someone with an absolutely distinctive set of skills, perspectives and experiences. So, find a career, or make one up, to work on the hardest problem that you feel most uniquely qualified to solve.
>
> **ZUBAIR JUNJUNIA, FOUNDER, ZNOTES EDUCATION**

Don't let others define you.

> **PETER DUFFY, CEO, MONEYSUPERMARKET GROUP**

Life is too short to compromise.

> Never take advice from someone who is telling you that you can't do something – there is always a way! Do what is right for you, when it is right for you.
>
> **DR ANASTASIA ALCOCK, PAEDIATRIC EMERGENCY MEDICINE CONSULTANT**

Invest in mentors with a small 'm'.

> I think many people obsess over the need for a formal 'Mentor' with a capital 'M' – which is so hard to a) identify and b) foster an enduring relationship with. I prefer informal 'mentors' (plural, lower case) – and, even better, the idea of us each building our 'personal board of advisors' (not that you'd necessarily term them that or 'recruit' them in that way!). My personal board consists of a selection of individuals I find inspiring – both professionally and personally. Some are much older, many are my peers, some much younger; some with similar backgrounds, some very, very different. Some are great for logistical, 'how to' advice, others for emotional support (having been there, done that). But with all, I'd say I share similar values. I frequently find that I have as much to offer them over the longer term as they, me. These relationships need to be fostered and invested in over the long term. I check in to see what they're up to and if I can support them in any way, sharing their big news with my network etc. – and they do the same. Helping them has actually been a huge source of professional development for me – realizing how much I have in fact learnt and enabling me to climb my own ladder that much faster. They're built and thrive on good karma and many of them have led to some of the greatest professional opportunities and revelations of my life.
>
> **JESSICA BUTCHER MBE, ENTREPRENEUR**

Doing the right thing is better than doing things exactly right.

Having been saved from the Holocaust by generous strangers, I determined early on that I would make mine a life worthy of being saved. So I try always to do the right thing, not just do things right in my perfectionist way. In my twenties, I started to battle against the sexism of the time and set up one of the first hi-tech companies in Britain as a flexible, family-friendly organization for women. Our first – and hence only – child Giles was profoundly autistic, which drove the remainder of my life as a venture philanthropist. I am still with my first husband and do not plan to retire.

DAME STEPHANIE
SHIRLEY,
BUSINESSWOMAN AND
PHILANTHROPIST

Pick your partner.

Choose who you decide to spend your life with very, very carefully, and I think this is especially true for women. Having the wrong life partner can really derail you and limit you and I see it all around me. If you have someone who supports and believes in you, when you don't even believe in yourself they become your biggest champion. I know that I would not be where I am today with my business if my partner had not seen in me something that I could not even conceive of in myself at that time. It's not that he did the work – I obviously did the work – but he created so many opportunities for support and I felt that I could ask him for that. So I think especially with younger women I would say choose who it is. I've spent plenty of time in my life with people who would have very happily limited my career to advance theirs.

MARYAM PASHA, DIRECTOR AND CURATOR, TEDXLONDON AND
TEDXLONDONWOMEN, AND DIRECTOR, X EQUALS

Hoover up knowledge.

Have a healthy degree of paranoia and embrace change as a constant. Do this and you'll know what's likely to happen, why it will happen and where you need to be when it happens.

WILL KING, ENTREPRENEUR AND FOUNDER, KING OF SHAVES

You drive you.

Decide what you want from your career. We spend a lot of time at work, so think about what's really important to you and what drives you. Be honest with yourself. It might be reaching the top job. It could be being in a great team – but great at what? Supporting one another, innovating, winning . . . ? Maybe your drive is providing an excellent service to each and every customer. Being clear about what you want and what particularly drives you will help you make the right choices and decide where you will and won't compromise.

DR PAULA FRANKLIN, CHIEF MEDICAL OFFICER, BUPA GROUP

Separate fear from uncertainty.

It is hard to separate uncertainty from fear – fear of the unknown, fear of what might happen, or what might not happen. One of the thoughts I carry with me (no doubt informed by the first twenty-five years of my career as a professional dancer and choreographer) is that artists are great at dealing with uncertainty, at being adaptable, flexible, tenacious and resilient, and at looking at things in new ways, making connections between ideas, things and people that others may fail to notice. We need this kind of mindset in uncertain times, especially in the midst of a global pandemic. We should all become better at holding things up for question, without the ever-present need for immediate certainty.

KENNETH THARP
CBE, BRITISH
DANCE ARTIST
AND FORMER CEO
OF THE PLACE

Chameleon is not a good look for a career.

Early in my career discrimination led me to contort myself into shapes that enabled me to fit into the space 'allowed' for me. I had grown to adapt like a chameleon, and change colour to suit my surroundings, and in so doing I had lost my identity. In my role as a leader for social good I now recognize the need to build self-trust, which requires being transparent and accountable, being personally vulnerable, taking risks, speaking up, talking about my failures and consciously choosing alignment with my values. I strongly believe that, in order to be part of a balanced, healthy society, we need to create opportunities for restitution, and that starts with knowing myself and learning to practise self-care and self-soothing.

POPPY JAMAN OBE, CEO, CITY MENTAL HEALTH ALLIANCE

Keep your head in the clouds and your feet on the ground.

In other words, try and regularly dream big, aim high, but at the same time take concrete, small steps forward. Do these things together and magic will happen. You can't control most things in your life and career, but you always have the freedom of your imagination and the ability to start something. Those are powerful forces. Use them.

BEN KEANE, CO-FOUNDER, REBEL BOOK CLUB

Your path will be fluid.

What you do and how you do it will evolve throughout the journey. So be bold, trust your instincts and have confidence in your decisions. If they don't work as you had hoped then you can learn from them, adapt and move forward knowing more than you did before.

TANSY HAAK, FOUNDER AND DESIGNER, KIND JEWELLERY

Just because you haven't, doesn't mean you can't.

There's a first time for everything. So say yes to new learning opportunities and make sure that five years' experience is not actually one year but repeated five times. And PS: when the going gets tough, remember you can't cry and whistle at the same time. So pucker up and blow!

STEVIE SPRING CBE, CHAIRMAN OF THE BRITISH COUNCIL AND MIND

Joy can be fleeting but authenticity prevails.

Find that golden intersection of what you're good at, what you feel strongly about and what brings you joy. I've found that the joy bit can be fleeting or inconsistent, especially in the beginning, but settles in with hard work and authenticity if you persevere.

SOPHIE SLATER, CO-FOUNDER OF BIRDSONG LONDON

An extra hour makes all the difference.

Spend your time wisely; we all have the same amount of time. If you take an extra hour every day of the week, that's a whole other working day each week to get ahead of others.

TOM CHAPMAN, FOUNDER OF THE LIONS BARBER COLLECTIVE

Go make some projects.

The career of 2020 and beyond is not a series of jobs with painful unemployment in between it's a series of projects. And if you can do a series of projects with one boss for the rest of your life, fine. If you can do projects with never having a boss, fine. But you make projects. The arc of your life can be defined by the scale and impact and quality of your projects, so go make some projects.

SETH GODIN, AUTHOR AND ENTREPRENEUR

Be more than an athlete – you are a long time retired.

I think the best advice came in two parts but joined together really well. From my father it was 'you should be more than an athlete', which really meant that he expected me to do other things than just be involved in sport. He was very keen that I had more to talk about than what training session I had just done and what was I going to do next. It made me realize that I always needed to be thinking about trying to find balance in my life. The second was from David Moorcroft, who told me after my third Games, 'you are a long time retired'. There are many parts to a career in wheelchair racing, such as GB representation but also all the road racing that we did away from the squad. I think it was useful to make me think about where the end point might be and also what I wanted to do next, although I had been thinking about that from the age of twenty-one.

BARONESS GREY-THOMPSON DBE, FORMER PARALYMPIAN, WELSH POLITICIAN AND TV PRESENTER

Ignore the 'not enough' voice in your head, it's the dreariest thing about you.

Dial down that noisy voice in your head questioning whether you're good enough, clever enough, eloquent enough, gorgeous enough or talented enough. That voice is the dreariest thing about you. Ignore it entirely and crack on!

RUTH IBEGBUNA, FOUNDER, RECLAIM AND THE ROOTS PROGRAMME

Don't set goals, set habits.

The only actual conspiracy you need to worry about is the fact that everyone is winging it and trying to pretend they're not. So, make it easy for everybody and talk in simple terms, be nice, smile big and try and make everyone feel good. Things open up when people start to relax. Life will be easier if people like you, but harder if they don't also respect you. Sometimes we can fight situations rather than for causes we believe in. If, when you've taken a step back, you still believe in your point of view, go for it. Most people follow the herd and haven't thought things through, which can be your opportunity. Just be sure you're not fighting for fighting's sake.

SIMON PITKEATHLEY, CEO, CAMDEN TOWN UNLIMITED

Don't dream big.

Don't dream big. Not always, anyway. Ambition is great for getting started on the career ladder but it can also give you tunnel vision. Taking time to reflect at every stage of your career is more important. If you just keep climbing, you'll end up miserable. Successful probably, rich maybe, but still miserable.

MATT RUDD, *SUNDAY TIMES* WRITER AND AUTHOR

We are the company we keep.

Find the best person in the room, and instead of wondering how to tear them down or outdo them – work out how to collaborate. We're known by the company we keep, and we're always better as collaborators than competitors.

SOPHIE WILLIAMS, ANTI-RACISM ADVOCATE, ACTIVIST AND AUTHOR

Find a place to be yourself, a place to belong.

Do something that brings you joy. Whether that's something you passionately believe in or an environment or company you feel at home in. Our work lives can't be separated from our lives . . . Find a place you can be yourself, a place to belong.

KATIE VANNECK-SMITH, CO-FOUNDER AND PUBLISHER, TORTOISE MEDIA

The person you need to impress the most is yourself.

Trust your gut instinct and don't be afraid to dream big. You'll meet many doubters along the way but the person you need to impress the most is yourself. Work hard, have fun but ultimately stay true to who you are.

BABITA SHARMA,
BBC TELEVISION
NEWSREADER

Don't wait until you are older, richer or wiser to discover your passions.

Life is wonderful. Life is valuable. Life is full of opportunities. But it is also short. So, don't wait until you are older, richer or wiser to discover your passions. Find out what you love, get cracking, and make sure that whatever it is that you do, it has a positive impact on our planet and makes the world a better place.

PAUL JOYNSON-HICKS MBE, PHOTOGRAPHER

Be OK with beans on toast for dinner again.

Something I see particularly in women is starting a business but trying to maintain everything as it was. Having a business, and especially getting one started, takes some serious graft and sacrifice and you can't do everything you did before and simply have a business on top. Of course, there will be less women in business if we're always doing it as a side project while juggling everything else. It took being OK with beans on toast for dinner again, my social life took a backseat, some serious conversations with my husband about better splitting everything that needed doing at home, and then I needed some serious conversations with myself that it was OK to love my work and the guilt was just a waste of energy that I didn't have. Most men who start businesses do not have to contend with those things.

STEPH DOUGLAS, CEO AND FOUNDER, DON'T BUY HER FLOWERS

Dare to dream.

The only thing that had a lasting impact on me from my English Literature classes was an excerpt from a poem by the great Irish poet William Butler Yeats: 'I have spread my dreams under your feet; Tread softly because you tread on my dreams.' So many people in business use the phrase, 'Let's not try and boil the ocean,' and my response is, 'Give it a go,' because if you don't, how do you know what is possible? Yoda from *Star Wars* summed it up perfectly when he said, 'Do or do not, there is no try,' when training Luke Skywalker in the ways of the force.

JONATHAN AUSTIN, FOUNDER AND CEO, BEST COMPANIES LTD

Learn from people you don't like.

I've learnt as much from the people I don't want to be like and the work culture I don't want to be part of as the ones that I do. All experiences should help shape the person you want to be and the career you want to build. Be true to yourself, your values, and no matter what happens in a day, you will have lived the day with authenticity and purpose.

CAROLINE RUSH, CEO, BRITISH FASHION COUNCIL

Never let the fear of failure stop you.

No one knows the future. The best we can do is give it our best shot. And do what you love as it's normally what you're best at!

JENNY COSTA, FOUNDER AND CEO, RUBIES IN THE RUBBLE

Say yes to opportunities even if you're not ready.

I was very lucky growing up with parents who did what they loved. My father was a musician and my mother a journalist. The only advice I ever got given was 'do whatever makes you happy'. I realize that this advice could go one of two ways with children but I was pretty self-motivated! My advice would be similar – do what you love. That way, you'll overcome obstacles (which are inevitable) and you'll also be prepared to work hard (also inevitable in order to be successful). If you don't know what you're passionate about then try lots of different things to decide what you do and don't like. Say yes to opportunities even if you don't think you're ready. Do what you love, with people who inspire you, and you won't work a day in your life.

GOLDIE SAYERS, FORMER BRITISH JAVELIN THROWER, OLYMPIC BRONZE MEDALLIST

Your network is your net worth

It is often quoted that your 'network is your net worth' and that is absolutely true, your network and relationships can help to enhance and define your future. Which means you have to be ready and willing to connect with a variety of people along the way – on and offline. We are firm believers in 'networking karma' so it is essential to network reciprocally; having the humility to ask for help and the willingness to actively offer help is the winning combination. Do not underestimate the importance of relationships, they are an essential component to a successful life, business or career.

BIANCA MILLER-COLE AND BYRON COLE, AUTHORS OF *SELF MADE* AND *THE BUSINESS SURVIVAL KIT*

Know your worth.

> There are four golden workplace rules that I try my best to follow whenever possible. Firstly, I'm fiercely against five- or ten-year career plans. Don't create a metric for success based on what you used to want. Always chase what you enjoy now and open yourself up to new opportunities whenever you see them. Secondly, always know your worth. There's a taboo around money, especially in the UK, designed to keep women in particular silent about pay gaps. Talking about money will help to smash this. Thirdly, don't be put off an industry because you don't see people like you at the top. Use that as motivation. That industry needs people like you. Go get it! Finally, failing is good. Failing teaches us and gives us an opportunity to pause, reflect and re-evaluate what is right for us. Don't be afraid of failing, embrace it.
>
> **LAURA CORYTON, BRITISH CAMPAIGNER, FEMINIST ACTIVIST AND AUTHOR**

Seek out the people who seem different.

> As in life, enjoying and succeeding at work is all about people. Be open, listen and put energy into building relationships, especially with people who seem the most different. Strong, personal relationships with people holding different ideas, experiences and abilities will not only provide you with a team of people to call upon when needed, but also broaden your own knowledge and approach and make work so much more interesting, fun and fulfilling.
>
> **KALI HAMERTON-STOVE, PROJECT DIRECTOR, THE GLASSHOUSE**

Purpose and passion matter most.

> We spend so much of our life at work, so think carefully about what culture you need in order for you to thrive at work and that will allow you to be true to yourself, as nothing is more exhausting than having to act differently. Find your purpose at work – what really motivates and drives you. If you are more passionate about what you are doing you are more likely to be more committed and therefore more likely to succeed.
>
> **KIRSTIE MACKEY OBE, MANAGING DIRECTOR, CITIZENSHIP AND CONSUMER AFFAIRS, BARCLAYS UK**

Make memories.

The beautiful thing about your career is that it is YOURS. Yours to shape, yours to enjoy and yours to celebrate. And seeing a career as a part of your purpose and as a reflection of your essence also makes it yours to protect. So as much as possible fill it with happy, kind, varied, vibrant, creative and rewarding activities (and memories).

YEWANDE AKINOLA MBE, CHARTERED ENGINEER AND TV PRESENTER

Follow your strongest heartbeat when faced with a fork in the road.

As trite as it might sound, I would urge everyone, at every point in their life, to always follow their strongest heartbeat when faced with a fork in their career journey. And to do so with confidence and full passion. There are many different drivers that will need to take centre stage at different points in our lives; following the sound of the loudest beating heart will always take you to a place you're proud to be in and have full ownership of. Don't have expectations of where you hope one step will take you to – it will rarely line up the laddered way you hope it will – but it might just open unknown and unlikely doors that reveal a world of unimagined possibility to you. A wise friend once told me that if the next move isn't a step into the unknown and uncomfortable, it can't be a step forward. Be brave – life is for the brave. There is no such thing as a perfect fit. Make the most of every opportunity and every open door that reveals itself to you. You may not walk through that open door now, but you might want to in a few years' time. I was told it wasn't possible to have the career I now have and that I would have to choose between being a barrister in private practice, working on the front line in international development and continuing pursuits in academia. When I left the Bar to pursue international development in conflict zones I was told it was career suicide, that I would never be able to come back to the Bar. Nonetheless I followed that heartbeat and left without looking back, embracing human rights in an entirely new career and learning new skills along the way. As it turned out, and when it worked for me, I was able to come back to the Bar in a stronger position, with a set of valued new skills. These unlikely unfamiliar steps helped me create a practice that could cohabit with my international work and support my work in academia at Oxford University. Thanks to ignoring the naysayers I have a thriving career that works perfectly for me – one that combines exciting litigation in private practice, international development, public speaking, academia and even has space for my love of literature. You can do absolutely anything and do it the way you want to as well. The impossible is always possible.

SANGEETHA IENGAR, AWARD-WINNING INTERNATIONAL HUMAN-RIGHTS BARRISTER

Be open to new experiences.

Make yourself more open to new experiences, challenges and people with different perspectives and backgrounds to your own. Find an issue you care about, work hard and collaborate with others to achieve your goals.

MICHELLE MITCHELL OBE, CHIEF EXECUTIVE AT CANCER RESEARCH UK

Leadership is a mindset and an attitude, not a job title.

Everyone can be a leader if they choose to be, it's a mindset and an attitude, not a job title or an exam to pass. How different and better might the world be if we developed leadership capabilities nearer the start of people's careers, instead of ten or twenty years later? To accelerate this leadership development, find yourself a mentor – aim as high as you can, and choose someone who behaves in a manner that you would like to replicate. If at first they say no, try flattery, it works every time.

RENÉ CARAYOL MBE, AUTHOR AND BROADCASTER

Online or offline you need boundaries, so set an alarm.

I work flexibly but crave boundaries. I've started putting an out-of-office on when I'm not working – to ease the unending guilt we carry when not 'on' 24/7. I've started being specific with details like 'doing bathtime' or 'on a run' to humanize the workplace and own my down-time, which is not something layered with guilt. It's essential to productivity. I've also found setting an alarm at the beginning and end of my working day gives a clear book-end to what I'm doing. Online or offline, you need boundaries.

ANNA WHITEHOUSE, FOUNDER, MOTHER PUKKA

In the words of Take That ... Someday soon this will all be someone else's dream.

Someone once told me that in life you are typically either a journey or a destination person. Either focused on the ultimate position or driven to enjoy every role along the way to its fullest. I am definitely a journey person and that drives the best advice I can share. Being able to enjoy every role you undertake, using it to provide learning and people connections as well as KPI achievement will greatly increase your chances of success. In my experience, being both happy and successful in each role you take through your career, even through life's inevitable ups and downs, is the best way to ensure personal and professional progression. If I ever stop enjoying my role, regardless of how well I'm doing, that has always been my signal to make a change. I love also to remember the words of Take That in 'Never Forget' – 'Someday soon this will all be someone else's dream' which reminds me we only have the privilege of each role we're in for a period of time and must ensure we are developing our successors to help them achieve their own dreams as we have ours.

CLARE CLOUGH,
UK MANAGING
DIRECTOR, PRET
A MANGER

You are the greatest project you will ever work on.

You are the greatest project that you will ever get to work on, so make time to pursue those things that spark a light in you. You will live a better story by doing so. Be patient with this process because it can often take years before you arrive at that one year that will completely transform your life for the better. And have the wisdom to unearth the lessons behind every setback. I promise you they are there, waiting to be understood so that they can help you to come back stronger.

SIMON ALEXANDER ONG, LIFE COACH AND BUSINESS STRATEGIST

Let the small stuff go.

Nobody in business purposely goes out to hurt. Most people are surviving and wanting to get through it at their best. If someone sends you a curt email, if someone's a bit abrupt, if someone is taking credit for your work, don't get hung up on that, you're just wasting your energy. Just go back, open up the dialogue. Be open. Be honest. Let the small stuff go. Focus on what you're doing and do it to your best.

MARY PORTAS, RETAIL CONSULTANT AND BROADCASTER

You don't need to know all the answers and you don't have to pretend that you do.

The single best lesson I've ever learnt is that you don't have to know all the answers and you don't have to pretend you do. Asking for help is the single greatest thing I've ever learnt . . . no human being is strong enough to solve these complicated problems by ourselves. We are very, very powerful in groups, we are very, very powerful as tribes, but we're pretty useless as individuals. So if you ask for help you're giving the opportunity for the tribe, friends and colleagues to serve, and that is the greatest gift you can give them.

SIMON SINEK, AUTHOR

Ambition and discomfort go hand in hand.

> If you are not uncomfortable a couple of times a month then you are not pushing yourself. We learn when we are uncomfortable as we're facing something we haven't done before, we're in an environment we haven't seen before, we are in a situation that's not familiar. All those things make you uncomfortable, and all those things enable you to learn and to grow. So, if you are ambitious it's OK to be uncomfortable, and if you're not, then you're not pushing yourself enough.

SHELLYE ARCHAMBEAU, FORTUNE 500 BOARD MEMBER,
FORMER CEO OF METRICSTREAM, ADVISOR AND AUTHOR

If you don't ask, you don't get.

> If you don't ask, you don't get – that's been my whole career in advertising and I think it's so true of this industry, it's really about reaching out, connecting with people but also being brave enough to put yourself out there.

NIRAN VINOD, CO-FOUNDER AND CREATIVE DIRECTOR, DEFT

Remember, everyone was a beginner once.

> Don't ever be afraid to ask questions or for help. Everyone was new to what they're doing at some point. It might feel uncomfortable, but sometimes it's necessary not only to do your job right, but also for personal and professional growth

FRANCESCA JAMES, CO-FOUNDER, GREAT BRITISH ENTREPRENEUR AWARDS

Experience is the way you figure out what you like.

> My biggest piece of advice is work experience. Getting hands-on experience is key and you get to figure out what you like and what you don't. Plus the contacts and connections you will make could be pivotal in your future career!

SARAH STIRK, SKY SPORTS TV PRESENTER

Build it and they will come. Have concrete faith in yourself and people will take a chance on you.

My career advice is stolen from *Field of Dreams* – if you build it, they will come. I've been offered a lot of very exciting opportunities as a freelance writer – but I reached a point when I realized I'd lost my sense of career direction; I'd just been saying yes to everything and I wasn't on the right path. I didn't even know how to get to the path. So I realized I had to start building and making the work I wanted from scratch. I started my literary interview podcast, *You're Booked*. I wrote several books – *How to be a Grown Up*, *The Sisterhood* and my first novel, *Insatiable*. I really had to wrestle with myself over *Insatiable*, because every time I sat down to work, a little voice said, 'You're wasting your time, you might not be any good at this, what if no one wants to publish it?' I had no confidence in my work. But I found it by thinking of all the times when I'd been in that situation before. I had built it, and they had come. And no one is going to come if they get to where the building should be and there aren't even any foundations! We need to demonstrate concrete faith in ourselves and our work before anyone else is going to take a chance on us.

DAISY BUCHANAN, WRITER AND PODCASTER

Speak what you seek, until you see what you say.

This quote helped me at a time in my career when I was feeling uncertain. My heart and my head weren't in sync and I didn't know what decision to make. I stumbled on this quote at exactly the right time. It gave me the clarity and the confidence to voice the hopes and ideas I'd been thinking to myself, and the more I did, the more of a reality they became. I don't think I would be where I am today if this quote hadn't found me along the way.

**HELEN TUPPER,
CEO AND
CO-FOUNDER,
AMAZING IF**

We are what we repeatedly do. Excellence, then, is not an act, but a habit.

I spent too much of my early career worrying about not being smart enough and comparing myself to other, 'smarter' people. I decided to stop worrying about 'smartness' and start worrying about how hard I work and how much effort and care I put in. This transformed how in control of my career I felt and I'm convinced I've achieved more and been braver as a result.

**SARAH ELLIS,
CO-FOUNDER,
AMAZING IF**

The End is the Beginning

You Coach You doesn't finish with a chapter titled 'Conclusion' for a reason: our careers are always a work-in-progress, and we never reach the point at which we're 'done' with learning. Every topic in this book is something you can keep practising and improving. We don't expect anyone to read a chapter on self-belief or relationships or resilience and think *I've got that all sorted now*. What we do hope is that you have lots of tools, techniques and ideas that you start applying and adapting for yourself. One of our favourite moments at work is when a reader or listener gets in touch to tell us that they've taken an idea we've shared and made it even better for themselves. You have our full permission to play and experiment with everything in this book and create your own toolkit to support you wherever your squiggly career takes you.

> *Learn to know yourself.*
> **NELSON MANDELA**

Put your energy and effort into what you can control: you

There are lots of things about your career that you can't predict or control. There are the big things we don't know, like what jobs will exist in the future or what skills we'll be learning in five years' time. Then there are the small things, like what mood our manager will come to work in today or how our priorities will change week to week. Work takes up a lot of our time and energy and we don't want to waste it trying to control the uncontrollable, as that is both an exhausting and thankless task. Instead, let's put our efforts into what we can control: ourselves.

Let's focus our efforts . . .

- ⤳ on recovering and learning from the small and big moments of difficulty in our days.
- ⤳ on our time at work being well spent.
- ⤳ on building our belief so we can explore our potential and survive setbacks.
- ⤳ on investing in a community of people who support our career.
- ⤳ on creating exciting opportunities to progress in our career.
- ⤳ on making progress towards a purpose that is motivating and meaningful.

Share what you know so everyone can succeed

There's room for everyone to succeed in squiggly careers. Sharing what you know not only helps other people to succeed but also helps you learn more. There are no 'secrets' to success; we all have ideas and knowledge to give and gain from each other's experience. The more generous we are, the more good we can all do. As Sarah's little boy Max frequently reminds her (mainly when he wants some chocolate), *sharing is caring.*

Acknowledgements

There was a risk that after the success of our first book, *The Squiggly Career, You Coach You* would suffer from 'difficult second album' syndrome. What we didn't anticipate was more than a year during which we barely saw each other and had to figure out how to pivot our business during and after a pandemic. It certainly put writing a second book into perspective! It was tempting at times to pause our plans for this book, and certainly after the zillionth Zoom call it was more than just tempting. What kept us going is the impact we could see Covid was having on everyone's careers. It accelerated trends that were already underway and made the need for accessible career support urgent and important. So we rolled up our sleeves, got gritty and kept going . . .

Get the right people on the bus and in the right seat.

JIM COLLINS

This book is an excellent example of what author and leadership expert Jim Collins calls *getting the right people on the bus*. The right people are the only reason that you're reading this book and our bus is brimming with brilliance:

Our family and friends who help us find the space to write, listen to our struggles and very practically 'borrow' our children when we're up against a deadline.

Our editors at Penguin, Celia and Lydia, who gave us the extra time we needed when we had our 'we're not going to make it' wobble and who read every word and completed every exercise to make sure what we wrote was as helpful for our readers as possible.

Sarah, our team manager, who joined to help us for a few weeks when we launched our first book and thank goodness hasn't got off the bus since. Sarah is the reason that we keep moving and make progress; without her there is no doubt we would have had to pull over in panic.

And we're so grateful we got on this bus together. Friendships that turn into brilliant business partnerships are rare, but we're very happy for ours to be the exception.

We want to finish this book where we started, by saying thank you to all our readers and listeners who bought a 'ticket' to get on the bus with us. We really appreciate your trust and support for the work that we do.

We hope *You Coach You* sparks a new way of approaching your career and creates a community of like-minded learners who can connect and support each other. We don't know exactly where our bus will end up, but we do know that the sign on the front will always say *making careers better for everyone*.

Thank you.

Sarah and Helen

Notes

1. https://hbr.org/2009/01/what-can-coaches-do-for-you
2. https://positivepsychology.com/daily-affirmations/
3. https://hbr.org/2018/01/what-self-awareness-really-is-and-how-to-cultivate-it
4. https://hbr.org/2016/07/what-great-listeners-actually-do
5. https://hbr.org/1957/09/listening-to-people
6. https://hbr.org/2020/06/a-plan-for-managing-constant-interruptions-at-work
7. https://hbr.org/2016/06/resilience-is-about-how-you-recharge-not-how-you-endure
8. https://hbr.org/2019/12/what-happens-when-your-career-becomes-your-whole-identity
9. www.bbc.com/worklife/article/20200821-the-strategy-that-turns-daydreams-into-reality
10. https://academic.oup.com/jcr/article/44/1/118/2736404
11. www.bbc.com/worklife/article/20191202-how-time-scarcity-makes-us-focus-on-low-value-tasks
12. www.healthline.com/health/mental-health/burnout-definition-world-health-organization
13. www.gallup.com/workplace/237059/employee-burnout-part-main-causes.aspx
14. https://hbr.org/2015/05/millennials-say-theyll-relocate-for-work-life-flexibility
15. https://hbr.org/2019/07/why-you-should-stop-trying-to-be-happy-at-work
16. https://expandedramblings.com/index.php/email-statistics/
17. https://hbr.org/2017/07/stop-the-meeting-madness
18. https://research.udemy.com/wp-content/uploads/2018/03/FINAL-Udemy-2018-Workplace-Distraction-Report.pdf
19. https://hbr.org/1999/11/management-time-whos-got-the-monkey
20. www.telegraph.co.uk/finance/jobs/11691728/Employees-waste-759-hours-each-year-due-to-workplace-distractions.html
21. www.webfx.com/blog/internet/music-productivity-infographic/

22. https://hbr.org/2013/11/emotional-agility
23. www.psychologytoday.com/gb/blog/finding-purpose/201810/what-actually-is-belief-and-why-is-it-so-hard-change
24. https://hbr.org/2012/09/to-succeed-forget-self-esteem.html
25. https://hbr.org/2018/09/give-yourself-a-break-the-power-of-self-compassion
26. www.jstor.org/stable/40063169?seq=1
27. https://hbr.org/2019/05/the-little-things-that-affect-our-work-relationships
28. https://journals.sagepub.com/doi/abs/10.1177/0146167208328062
29. www.cse.wustl.edu/~m.neumann/fl2017/cse316/materials/strength_of_weak_ties.pdf
30. https://herminiaibarra.com/reinventing-your-career-in-the-time-of-coronavirus/
31. https://greatergood.berkeley.edu/article/item/how_grateful_are_americans
32. www.gallup.com/workplace/236570/employees-lot-managers.aspx
33. https://fortune.com/2015/04/02/quit-reasons/
34. https://hbr.org/2018/01/why-we-should-be-disagreeing-more-at-work
35. https://hbr.org/2018/09/what-to-do-if-theres-no-clear-career-path-for-you-at-your-company
36. www.psychologytoday.com/gb/articles/201711/the-comparison-trap
37. https://hbr.org/1993/09/why-incentive-plans-cannot-work
38. www.bbc.co.uk/news/health-27393057
39. www.pewforum.org/2018/11/20/where-americans-find-meaning-in-life/
40. www.mckinsey.com/business-functions/organization/our-insights/covid-19-and-the-employee-experience-how-leaders-can-seize-the-moment
41. www.researchgate.net/publication/304087988_The_Search_for_Purpose_in_Life_An_Exploration_of_Purpose_the_Search_Process_and_Purpose_Anxiety
42. https://hbr.org/2020/11/what-you-should-follow-instead-of-your-passion

Index

AAA 148–9
Achor, Shawn 55
acquaintances 164, 174–5
action 11, 36, 37
    see also COACH; ideas for action
activators 184–7, 190
adversity 42, 67
    audit 59–60
    building bridges to action 62
    reflections 62–3
Aesop 173
Akinola, Yewande 274
Alcock, Anastasia 262
Alexander, Simon 278
Allcott, Graham 111–12
Allen, David 109
Amazing If 2
ambition 225, 226
Anderson, Gillian 254
Angelou, Maya 117
anxiety, purpose 226
appreciate, acknowledge and assess
    148–9
Archambeau, Shellye 279
Ardern, Jacinda 234
Austin, Jonathan 271
autopilot 88, 89
avoiders 184–7, 190

Balding, Clare 260
Bandura, Albert 119–20

Banksy 55
beginners' belief 152
beliefs 118–19
    changing 131–2, 133
Bergiers, Dominique 235
best friend 18–19
Beyoncé 40, 70
Bishop, Cath 261
blisters 250, 251
boredom 88, 89
borrowed belief 147
Bradford, David 157–8
Branson, Richard 195
brief moments of discomfort (BMDs)
    141–2
Brown, Brené 234
Buchanan, Daisy 280
Buddha 127
Buffett, Warren 163
burnout 74–5
busyness 73–4
Butcher, Jessica 262

Cable, Dan 5, 223, 229, 250–51, 253
Campbell, Natalie 227
can-if method 217–18
Carayol, René 276
career challenges 4–5, 38–9
    progression 193–220
    purpose 223–53
    relationships 157–90

career challenges (*cont.*)
  resilience 41–70
  self-belief 117–55
  time 73–114
career community 164–75, 190
career comparison 118
career confidants 164, 165–7
career connections 19, 165, 170–74
career conversations 3
career counsel 164, 165, 167–70
careers 1–2, 283–4
  advice from all areas 6, 255–81
casual acquaintances 164, 174–5
Catmull, Ed 64
challenge-and-build approach 170
challenging work 90–91
Chapman, Tom 267
Chen, Serena 120
Christopher Robin 116, 155
Cirillo, Francesco 107
clarity 36, 37
  see also COACH
Clifton, Rita 155
Clough, Clare 277
COACH 34, 36–8
  progression 219
  purpose 252
  relationships 189
  resilience 69
  self-belief 154
  time 113
coach yourself questions *see* questions
coaching 1–2
  catch-22 2
  democratizing 2–3
coaching yourself 2–3, 8, 11–12, 283–4
  beyond the book 7
  career challenges 4–5, 38–9
  mindset 2, 11, 12–20
  practising 6
  progression 193–220
  purpose 223–53
  relationships 157–90
  resilience 41–70

self-belief 117–55
skillset 2–3, 11, 21–33
time 73–114
toolkit 4, 11, 33–9
You Coach You community 7–8
cognitive diversity 159
Cohen-Hatton, Sabrina 259
Cole, Byron 272
Collins, Jim 76
Collins, Zoe 256
comfort zone 139, 155
comparison curse 118
Condry, John 196
confidants 164, 165–70
confidence 36, 37, 39
  see also COACH
conflict
  constructive 184–7
  difficult people 178–83
connections 164, 165, 170–74
Connolly, Billy 149
consensus seeking circle 180, 182–3, 190
constant calibration 104
constraints 216–18
constructive conflict 184–7
Copeland, Misty 54
Coryton, Laura 273
Costa, Jenny 272
counsel 164, 165
courage zone 139, 155
  scary scenarios 140
courageous conversations 176
Cousins, Margaret 167
Covey, Stephen 74
creating a new role 204
critic creep 17–20, 53, 134–5
critical feedback 148–9
Csikszentmihalyi, Mihaly 87

da Vinci, Leonardo 235
Dahl, Roald 9
Daisley, Bruce 23–4
data based diamond 180, 182–3, 190

David, Susan 117–18
Day, Elizabeth 120
day theming 109–110
Deaton, Angus 118
Didion, Joan 143, 147
difference 159, 190
   and friction 178–88, 190
difficult people 39, 178–88
difficulty 120
direction 224, 225
Disney, Walt 192, 220
Disraeli, Benjamin 221
distance 159–60, 190
distraction downfalls 86, 93,
      97–9, 114
dive deeper 26–7
diversity 159
doers 15–17
doing 123, 125, 155
   comfort vs courage zone 139
   creating your courage zone 139
   scary scenarios 140
   small actions to #bemoretortoise 141
donate 159, 160, 190
Douglas, Steph 271
Drucker, Peter 86
Duffy, Peter 262
Dunbar, Robert 164
Dweck, Carol 12

effort 88, 89
Einstein, Albert 28
Ellis, Katherine 234
empathy 176–8
encouragement 120
energy states 87–9
   and environment at work 93
enforced wait 217
enmeshment 57
environment 93
eudemonic happiness 224
Eurich, Tasha 21–2
even better if 91
explorer questions 32

facts 26, 27
Fast Company 10
favours 173–4
fears 27
feedback
   critical 148–9
   flow 91
feedback friends 23–4
feel-good folder 150
feelings 26, 27
Field of Dreams 280
15 counsel 164, 165, 167–70
50 connections 164, 165, 170–74
first person vs fly-on-the-wall 155
5 confidants 164, 165–7
five-minute favour 173–4
fixed mindset 12–15
flow 86, 87–9, 95
   feeding 89–93
   finding flow friends 89, 94
   minimizing flow foes 89, 93
Ford, Ashley C. 126
Franklin, Paula 264
friction 97–9
   fixing 190
frogs 109
future, imagining options 63, 65–6

Gallo, Amy 158, 162, 184, 187–8, 190
Garland, Judy 118
Gates, Melinda 191
Gautama Buddha 127
George, Rob 234
Getting Things Done (GTD) 109
Gibson, Kerry Roberts 158–9
Gielan, Michelle 55
Gilbert, Elizabeth 71
givers 160, 243
goalden hour 108
Godin, Seth 267
Gossage, Lucy 119, 121
Granovetter, Mark 160
Grant, Adam 160, 243
Grant, Heidi 120

Grey-Thompson, Baroness 267
growth mindset 12, 14–15
guess what? 233–4

Haak, Tansy 266
Halligan, Peter 118
Hamerton-Stove, Kali 273
happiness 224
hard to do's 209
Hawn, Goldie 243
heated hexagon 180, 182–3, 190
Heffernan, Margaret 49, 158, 159,
    210, 255
help 36, 37
    asking for 51–2, 67–8
    see also COACH; support
helper's high 243
150 acquiantances 164, 174–5

Ibegbuna, Ruth 268
ideas for action 34, 36
    progression 215
    purpose 232–4, 236, 239, 244–6
    relationships 166, 167, 169–70, 173–4,
        176, 177, 178, 185, 186, 187
    resilience 50, 51–2, 53, 54, 55–6, 57–8
    self-belief 134–6, 138, 141–2, 147,
        148–9, 150, 152
    time 90, 91, 92, 93, 94, 97–9
IDEO 210
Iengar, Sangeetha 275
if/then sequence statements 84–6
imagining options 63, 65–6, 70
imposter syndrome 152–3
inner critic 17–20, 53, 134–5
Instagram 7
interruption insight 25–6
investigator questions 31–2

Jaman, Poppy 266
James, Francesca 279
Jenkins, Tiffany 74
Jobs, Steve 136
Johnson, Dwayne 48

Jordan, Michael 67
Joynson-Hicks, Paul 271
Junjunia, Zubair 262

Kahneman, Daniel 118
Keane, Ben 266
Keller, Helen 67
Kelly, Colin 217
King, Kanya 256
King, Martin Luther, Jr 110
King, Will 264
Knowles, Beyoncé 40, 70
Kross, Ethan 134, 135
Krznaric, Roman 177, 225

Lady Gaga 139
Lambert, Linda 3
Lane-Fox, Martha 70, 256
Lawton, Emma 260
learning opportunities 205
Lennon, John 115
Leonardo da Vinci 235
Levinson, Ben 258
limiting lenses 128–9, 130, 133, 155
limitless lenses 130, 133, 155
listening to yourself 21, 24–8

McGregor, Heather 258
Mackey, Kirstie 273
managers
    disagreeing with 187–8
    repairing relationships with 39,
        175–8
managing your monkeys 95–6, 114
Markle, Meghan 57
mastery 119
meaning mentors 239
meaning meter 235–6, 253
meaningful goals 90
meaningful work 39, 235
    maximizing your moments 236–47,
        253
    meaning meter 235–6, 253
meetings 75, 111–12

mental contrasting 66
mentors 67–8, 262
    meaning mentors 239
    see also role models
middle-ground mediators 187, 190
Miller-Cole, Bianca 272
Milne, A. A. 116, 155
mind-map 230–34, 253
mindset 2, 11, 12
    critic creep 17–20
    magnets 12–15
    stubbornly adaptive 217
    thinkers and doers 15–17
Mitchell, Michelle 276
modelling 119
Moffat, Steven 62
monk mode 107
monkeys 95–6, 114
Moorcroft, David 267
Morgan, Adam 198, 216–18
Murphy, Kate 22
music mindset 108–9

Nadella, Satya 222, 253
Narcos 151
Netflix work—life documentary
        100–102, 114
Newport, Cal 74
Nichols, Ralph 24
Nike 226
no, saying 136–8
Nooyi, Indra 234
not going to plan 151–2

Os, 3 29–31
Obama, Barack 43
Obama, Michelle 1
Odedra, Kajal 46, 67–8, 239
Oettingen, Gabriele 66
O'Leary, Eithne 51
Oncken, William 95
one at a time questions 29–30
open questions 29
optimism 49–50

options 36, 37
    see also COACH
out of your depth 147–8
ownership questions 31

Ps of pessimism, 3 49–50
Pang, Alex 55
Pasha, Maryam 264
Pasricha, Neil 57
passion 250, 273
pauses 22–3
Pennebaker, James W. 143
Perel, Esther 157
perfection 225, 226
Perry, Grayson 234
personal pride 92
pessimism 49–50
pessimistic purpose 232–3
Pitkeathley, Simon 269
planets of progression 203–4
podcasts 7
pomodoro technique 107
Portas, Mary 278
positive people impact 236, 243–7
positive prompts 34, 35
    progression 196–7
    purpose 228–9
    relationships 161
    resilience 44–5
    self-belief 121–2
    time 77–8
press pause 22–3
Price, Catherine 148
pride 92
priorities 208
proactive progression 193–4
productivity partners 108
progression 4, 39, 193, 194, 220
    ask our expert 216–18
    COACH 219
    meaning 199–202
    owning your career 194
    possibilities 202–6, 220
    prioritizing 206–9, 220

progression (*cont.*)
  proactive 193–4
  progression pressure vs progressing at
    your own pace 196
  prototyping 210–213, 220
  ready-made rewards vs personalized
    progression 196
  securing support 214–16
  self-supporting statements 20
  thinking traps and positive prompts
    196–7
  and time 114
prototyping 210–213
purpose 4, 39, 223, 253, 273
  ask our expert 250–51
  COACH 252
  definitions 224–5
  exploring 230–35
  finding purpose from our work 223–4
  maximizing your moments of
    meaning 236–47
  meaning meter 235–6
  mind-map 230–34, 253
  principles 225–6
  purpose anxiety 226
  purpose fit 236, 237, 240–42, 253
  self-supporting statements 20
  a sense of direction 224
  thinking traps and positive prompts
    228–9
  work-in-progress statements 234–5
  You Create You 248
puzzle pieces 102–4

questions 21, 29, 34, 35
  the 3 Os 29–31
  the five connected whys 32–3
  investigator and explorer questions 31–2
  progression 220
  purpose 253
  relationships 190
  resilience 70
  self-belief 145–6, 155
  time 114

Rainey, Larissa 226
Rashford, Marcus 234
ready-made rewards 196
redundancy 149–51
relationships 4, 39, 157, 190, 272
  ask our expert 187–8
  career community 164–75
  COACH 189
  difference 159
  distance 159–60
  donate 160
  repairing 158–9, 175–88
  rewriting 157–8
  self-supporting statements 20
  thinking traps and positive prompts
    161
resilience 4, 39, 41, 70
  adversity audit 59–60
  ask our expert 67–8
  COACH 69
  mental time-travel 62–6
  range 42, 49, 70
  rating 46–7, 49, 70
  reactions 60–61
  reflections 62–3
  reserves 41–2, 49–58, 70
  resetting 42, 44
  role models 54
  self-supporting statements 20
  thinking traps and positive prompts
    44–5
rest and recovery 55–6
role models
  purpose 233–4
  resilience 54–5
Roots, Levi 256
Rubin, Theodore 224
Rudd, Matt 269
Rudoe, Laura 260
Rush, Caroline 272

Sandberg, Sheryl 193
Sayers, Goldie 272
saying 123, 124–5, 155

saying no 136–8
self-talk 134–6
scary scenarios 140–41
Schinoff, Beth 158–9
scribbling 6
Sebag-Montefiore, Clarissa 225
Seeger, Pete 169
self-awareness 11, 21–4
self-belief 4, 39, 117, 118–19, 155
    ask our expert 150–51, 152–3
    building blocks 123–6, 155
    COACH 154
    comparison curse 118
    doing 123, 125, 139–42
    saying 123, 124–5, 134–8
    self-belief surgery 143, 147–53
    self-doubt 117–18
    self-supporting statements 20, 150
    setbacks 143–6
    sources of 119–21
    thinking 123, 124, 125, 128–33
    thinking traps and positive prompts
        121–2
self-coaching see coaching yourself
self-compassion 120
self-doubt 117–18, 119, 120, 121
self-interruptions 25–6
self-supporting statements 18,
        19–20, 150
self-talk 134–6
Seligman, Martin 49, 53, 250
Seneca 75
setbacks 143
    coach yourself questions 145–6
    stories 143–4, 155
Shackell, Sherilyn 239
shared problem solving 166
sharing 284
Sharma, Babita 270
shiny objects 208
Shirley, Stephanie 263
Siddhartha Gautama 127
sideways move 205
Sinek, Simon 51, 278

skillset 2–3, 11, 21
    listening to yourself 24–7
    questioning 29–33
    self-awareness 21–4
Slater, Sophie 267
Smith, Maggie (poet) 249
Socrates 73
solutions 166
SORT framework 176
sounding board 166
Spielberg, Steven 24
spot the difference 169–70
Spring, Stevie 266
squiggly careers 1–2
Squiggly Careers podcast 7
Star Wars 271
Steinem, Gloria 63
Stirk, Sarah 279
stop 208–9
stories 143–4
Storr, Farrah 141
strengths 236, 237
    fuel your frequency 238–9
    spotlight 237–8
strong ties 159–60
stubbornly adaptive mindset 217
successes 53
support
    career confidants 166
    career connections 174
    progression 214–16
    repairing relationships 186
    resilience 54
swallowing the frog 109
switch-off Sundays 148
switching positions 177
Syed, Matthew 159

Take That 277
takers 160
talkative triangle 180, 182–3, 190
task:time ratio 81–3, 114
task batching 109–110
templates 110

10x help 51–2
thank yous 167
Tharp, Kenneth 265
thinkers and doers 15–17
thinking 123, 124, 125, 128, 155
    changing our beliefs 131–2, 133
    limiting lenses 128–9
    limiting to limitless lens 130, 133
thinking traps 34–5
    progression 196–7
    purpose 228–9
    relationships 161
    resilience 44–5
    self-belief 121–2
    time 77–8
thoughtful thank yous 167
time 4, 39, 73, 114
    ask our expert 111–12
    beyond time management 110
    COACH 113
    coach yourself 78
    how we feel about 79–84
    moving beyond busy 73–4
    self-supporting statements 20
    task : time ratio 81–3, 114
    ten time tactics 107–110
    thinking traps and positive prompts
        77–8
    time management myths 76
    time ratio 81–3
    trade-offs 81, 84–6, 114
    trade-ups 81, 86–99
    well spent or wasted 75
    work—life fit 74–5, 99–106
time blocking 109–110
to-think lists 107–8
Tolkien, J. R. R. 72, 114
toolkit see You Coach You toolkit
tortoises 140–41
trade-offs, time 81, 84–6, 114
trade-ups, time 81, 86–99

Tweddell, Eleanor 123, 150–51
two-minute rule 109

understudy skills 178
Uviebinené, Elizabeth 5, 123, 152–3

Vanneck-Smith, Katie 269
Vinod, Niran 279
volunteering 205–6

wabi-sabi 251
Wambach, Abby 156, 190
Wass, Donald 95
weak ties 159–60
websites 8
what next? 66, 70
Whatley, James 174
what's working well 91
Whitehouse, Anna 276
why 32–3
Williams, Sophie 269
Windust, Jamie 258
wishful thinking 66, 70
Wittgenstein, Ludwig 42
work redesign 205
work—life fit 39, 74–5, 99–106, 114
work-in-progress 225, 226
work-in-progress purpose statements
        234–5, 253
world outside work 57–8
Wright, Ian 257
write a letter to yourself 152

Yeats, William Butler 271
You Coach You community 7–8
You Coach You toolkit 4, 11, 33–4
    see also COACH; ideas for action;
        positive prompts; questions;
        thinking traps
You Create You 248
Young, James 7

My Notes

COACH

Clarity – what is your coaching challenge?

Options – what options could you explore?

Action – what actions will you take?

Confidence – how confident are you about taking those actions?

Help – what help do you need to overcome your challenge?

COACH

Clarity – what is your coaching challenge?

Options – what options could you explore?

Action – what actions will you take?

Confidence – how confident are you about taking those actions?

Help – what help do you need to overcome your challenge?

COACH

Clarity – what is your coaching challenge?

Options – what options could you explore?

Action – what actions will you take?

Confidence – how confident are you about taking those actions?

Help – what help do you need to overcome your challenge?

COACH

Clarity – what is your coaching challenge?

Options – what options could you explore?

Action – what actions will you take?

Confidence – how confident are you about taking those actions?

Help – what help do you need to overcome your challenge?

COACH

Clarity – what is your coaching challenge?

Options – what options could you explore?

Action – what actions will you take?

Confidence – how confident are you about taking those actions?

Help – what help do you need to overcome your challenge?

COACH

Clarity – what is your coaching challenge?

Options – what options could you explore?

Action – what actions will you take?

Confidence – how confident are you about taking those actions?

Help – what help do you need to overcome your challenge?